LIVING

ALSO BY ILCHI LEE

The Call of Sedona

Change

The Solar Body

Healing Society

The Twelve Enlightenments for Healing Society

Brain Wave Vibration

In Full Bloom

Principles of Brain Management

Healing Chakras

Mago's Dream

Human Technology

LifeParticle Meditation

LIVING

TAO

TIMELESS PRINCIPLES
FOR EVERYDAY
ENLIGHTENMENT

ILCHI LEE

BEST
LIFE
MEDIA

Best Life Media
459 N. Gilbert Road, C210
Gilbert, AZ 85234
www.bestlifemedia.com

First paperback edition: December 2015
Library of Congress Control Number: 2015955641
ISBN-13: 978-1-935127-83-3

With gratitude to the ancient teachers of Korean Tao tradition who allowed me to expand my experiences in the light of the great legacy of this knowledge.

CONTENTS

INTRODUCTION

Sharing the Flower of the Tao

FROM THE TIME I WAS YOUNG, I've spent a great deal of time wandering in search of the meaning of life. In my late teens, I often went to a mountain behind our village where people were rarely seen. I lay down on the ground and looked up into the dark night sky. A strange feeling—I don't know whether it was anger, frustration, sadness, or longing—would rise from somewhere deep in my mind while I was lying there, and, without even realizing it, I would suddenly jump up and shout at the sky.

"Who brought me into this world without my permission?" I yelled. "If you caused me to be born, then shouldn't you at least tell me why I should live?"

To help quiet my restless mind, I immersed myself in martial arts like Taekwondo and Hapkido, working myself to total exhaustion to forget that feeling of emptiness. When I emerged from my youth, with its memories of mostly confusion and wandering, I graduated from college, got a decent job, and even started a wonderful family. But I was not happy; living my life without knowing why caused me unendurable pain.

I voraciously read Western and Eastern books on the spiritual world, hoping to find the reason I should go on living. I studied Eastern medicine to learn about my body and even wandered in search of a teacher to liberate me from the mental anguish of not knowing why I should live. Fascinated by breathing and meditation, I even devoted myself to going into the mountains at dawn every day to train alone. I still could not find the answers.

In 1980, when I was thirty years old, I turned my back on everything in the world and, alone, went up Mt. Moak in Jeonju, South Korea. And, at the risk of my life, I experienced the Tao through twenty-one days of ascetic practice. That experience saved me from all the doubt and suffering of my life. I awakened to the truth that the cosmic life energy, which grants life to everything in heaven and earth and overflows throughout the universe, is who I really am. I realized that what was born into this life was merely my physical body, and that my true self had been in existence since before I received this body. I obtained the self-realization that I am eternally self-existing life: the Tao.

Thirty-five years have flown by since then. During that time, to bring the Tao that I experienced to many people, I have combined brain science with traditional Korean Sundo philosophy and mind-body training methods to develop many educational and training programs, such as Brain Education and Body & Brain Yoga. I've opened meditation centers all over the world for teaching these programs; I've founded many educational institutions, including two universities, and I've written about forty books.

The Tao is the very heart and center of my enlightenment and teachings. Of all the books I've written so far, this one will deal most directly and most in-depth with the Tao.

What, then, is the Tao? What is it about the Tao that has caused countless people, now and in ancient times, to try so hard to obtain it? What is it about the Tao that has ceaselessly captivated the hearts and minds of human beings?

The Tao is the ultimate truth and substance of life. It is what all of humanity's spiritual seekers have been pursuing, and it is complete oneness. It is the principle of life energy flowing behind all things in the cosmos, and it is the ultimate wholeness to which all things, on becoming

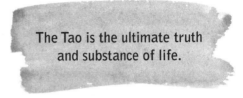

The Tao is the ultimate truth and substance of life.

one, return. Although it is all things in existence, the Tao is also the source and background that causes them to exist.

The word Tao is commonly written in Chinese characters like this: 道. This character contains the meanings of way, truth, and principle. Without fail, Lao Tzu is the person who comes up in discussions of the Tao. Lao Tzu is known as the philosopher who established and developed Taoist thought in ancient China 2500 years ago. Lao Tzu's *Tao Te Ching* is considered the greatest scripture of Taoism and contains the principles of nature and life in a short text made up of around 5000 characters in 81 chapters or sections. The *Tao Te Ching* has been translated into more languages worldwide than any book except the Bible. Just the commentaries that have come out of China on the *Tao Te Ching* are said to number in the hundreds of volumes.

Because of the influence of Lao Tzu's *Tao Te Ching*, many people think that the Tao belongs to China. In most ancient East Asian countries, however, the Tao was an important cultural and spiritual tradition, a normal part of life. Although it's clear that the word Tao is from an Eastern language, the Tao does not belong to the East alone. Even before the word existed, the Tao is something that has always existed fully, transcending the limitations of space and time comprehensible to humans.

I have little interest in understanding the Tao on a conceptual and intellectual level. For the Tao is not to be found in words. My interest is in how to feel and become one with the Tao. We must guard against the Tao being nothing more than a superficial idea, a spiritual accessory that fails to become part of our lives.

The purpose of this book is not to provide an emergency prescription or cure-all to solve all your problems in an instant. The purpose of this book is to methodically teach you a path to the Tao through twelve important topics, each of which is described in a separate chapter, and to inspire you with a passion for living a life of oneness with the Tao.

The path to the Tao introduced in this book is rooted in my personal experience and in Sundo, which is Korea's own millennia-old tradition of mind-body training. Sundo existed before Taoism and Buddhism were prevalent, and, although it influenced and was influenced by other spiritual traditions, it developed completely independently.

The core philosophy of Sundo is found in complete oneness with the Tao and is expressed in the ancient Korean scripture *Chun Bu Kyung* as follows: Bon Shim Bon Tae Yang Ang Myung, In Joong Chun Ji Il. This means, "Our true nature is like the sun and seeks the brightness; we find heaven and earth are one in humanity."

As the Chun Bu Kyung says, all humans have an inner longing to know their true nature, the Tao. Human bodies contain a complete Tao sense and a system through which they can feel and see the Tao. That sense is an energy sense for feeling and using the energy present in our bodies and in the universe, and the system is an energy system similar to the Hindu system of *chakras* (called *Dahnjon* in Korean) and includes awareness of meridians in our bodies. Energy principles and practices also exist that allow us to develop our energy sense and system. And, most important, we have a destination that our energy ultimately seeks. I believe that the ultimate destination is the growth and completion of the soul. To that end, in this book, I will introduce methods for studying the Tao through energy principles, practice, and living.

> Human bodies contain a complete Tao sense and a system through which they can feel and see the Tao.

The Tao is not something that can be known through words or knowledge. To know the Tao, you have to acquire a sense for life with your body, allowing yourself to feel the rhythm and flow of the Tao. Additionally, you must have eyes for watching yourself honestly and dispassionately, and you must learn how to ceaselessly let go of your fixed ideas about the world. What's more, just because you have known the Tao once does not mean yours becomes a Tao life. The Tao life can be called a practice of cultivating one's self that stretches across an entire lifetime of realizing the principles of the Tao.

When people think of spiritual practice, they usually think of strict discipline and restrictions, Buddhist priests in ink-stained robes, or monasteries cut off from the world. True spiritual practice is far removed from such things. Spiritual practice is a precious jewel we must all accept and cultivate as a part of our lives, to make our lives more meaningful and fulfilling. This book will have done its job if, when you close the cover on the final chapter, you realize that life is ultimately a spiritual practice for becoming one with the Tao, and if you have a serious desire to engage in spiritual practice.

When I've lectured on the Tao, I've been in the habit of carrying a golden rose to my first meeting with audience members. I've started our discussions like this:

I've brought a golden flower today. This flower symbolizes the Tao. Although it's one flower, just as the one moon shines its light on countless lakes, so, too, will this one flower be reflected in the lakes of your minds.

I have brought my heart with me, and you have brought your hearts here, too. Hearts and minds now meet as one.

I offer you this flower. Although the flower has now left my hands, it remains in my mind. And it is now in your mind. I've given you the flower. You have accepted it, and that is enough.

The Tao is a flower that never wilts. Though countless people pick it and take it with them, the flower of the Tao will always blossom anew.

I'd also like to offer the same golden rose to you, who is just starting to read this book. It's my heart, and a flower of the Tao. I'm putting my heart into it as I write these words, and you are putting your heart into it as you read them. Our hearts are now resonating with a desire to know, feel, and share the Tao.

It's not easy to share the Tao through words, which cannot

help but be limited. When you read this book, I would rather you feel the heart and energy I put into it than try to understand the meanings of each of its words and sentences. When your mind and mine become one, a sense for life develops, and that sense will be a dependable friend on your journey toward the Tao.

May our minds meet as one, causing the flames of our lives to burn brighter and, as it receives the warmth of that energy, may the flower of the Tao bloom fully in your heart.

Ilchi Lee
August 2015 in Sedona

CHAPTER ONE
Seeing the Tao

HAVE YOU EVER LOOKED AT A BEAUTIFUL FLOWER and been awed by life? Have you ever looked up at the stars in the night sky and trembled before the infinite spaces of the cosmos? Have you shed tears because you were deeply moved by the story of someone who practiced unconditional love? And, have you ever asked who am I, why am I here?

All these moments are our expressions of thirst for the Tao. They are also the moments we feel something after getting a glimpse of the Tao. In those moments when you encounter that small part of the Tao, you get a burst of inspiration, your heart swells without any reason, and, occasionally, you have a great realization that becomes a turning point in your life. In those moments, you experience a vague feeling that a sacred design, not to be imitated by even the most superior human intellect, exists in the universe.

Everyone has a desire to become one with the Tao; that is, everyone has a seeker's heart. The Tao is the background and motivating power of everything that exists in the world. It is also the world and everything in it. Our lives are part of the Tao and, therefore, we long for the Tao the way a fish longs for the ocean.

This thirst for the Tao is a power that, generation after generation, has pushed many to search for the ultimate meaning of life. It is also the power that has moved great scientists, writers, and artists to immerse themselves in a lifetime of research and creative activity. Great scientists discover the laws and principles governing the world through objective numbers and formulas; great poets sing of the world of the Tao through language; and great artists express inspiration concerning the Tao through images.

Longing for the Tao does not come to us only in moments of joy and awe. The opposite is actually much more frequent. You have probably had times when, on the outside, everything seemed to be going well, but one day, your heart suddenly felt empty and everything felt pointless. You might have awakened in the middle of the night and had trouble sleeping because a slew of questions about life were suddenly racing through your mind. Whether or not our health, occupations, or personal relationships are satisfying, these questions

> We long for the Tao the way a fish longs for the ocean.

lie under the surface of our busy, churning lives: Am I happy now? Do I have a direction or goal in my life? What in the world does all this mean?

You never need to be afraid when such moments come to you. It is in those moments when the roots of our lives are shaken, when we get the feeling that we have no direction, and when a sense of emptiness and futility washes over us that the thirst for the Tao within us raises its head. The seed of the seeker's heart sprouts in the rich soil of those feelings of emptiness and futility.

Perhaps you've said, or thought, "I have no interest in seeking truth. I simply want to live a life that's a little happier and fuller." But if you look deeply into your pursuit of a life that is more meaningful and better, you'll find that, ultimately, it too is a form of the seeker's heart. This is because, when seeking to create a genuinely happy and fulfilling life, material satisfaction alone cannot satisfy. You are someone who longs to know something greater and more fundamental to satisfy the thirst you feel in your daily, superficial life. Otherwise, you wouldn't ever have picked up this book. You can't really say exactly what it is, but you're searching for something meaningful. That thing you can't quite describe is the Tao. Your longing for it is the seeker's heart.

This seeker's heart is very important in the course of becoming one with the Tao. This is because, although everyone has that seeker's heart, when you acknowledge, hold precious, and develop that thirst for the Tao, your eyes open to see the Tao. Just as a hen uses her body heat to warm her clutch of eggs, you must continually increase the temperature of your pure longing for the Tao. Just as a glass of cold water is sweeter than any pricey drink to a person long parched by thirst, and just as the dry desert ground absorbs long-awaited rain, so too the whole body can absorb a glass of water in an instant. The deeper your longing for the Tao, the more powerful your encounter with it will be.

Consider precious your fundamental questions about life. Love that heart that holds doubt: Is this really all there is? Continue to dig into that mind. When your thirst for the Tao grows sharper and sharper and, like an arrow, pierces your soul, your eyes for seeing the Tao will start to open, like a chick breaking through its shell to emerge from its egg.

Seeing the Tao

There is something you should be wary of when you want to know what the Tao is: approaching the Tao through knowledge. We have continuously filled our heads with countless forms of artificial knowledge and information. We have been trained, through our education system, to see and judge life—and the world—by a standard measure of knowledge. Our eyes for seeing the essence of things have been clouded by that artificial knowledge and information.

The Tao is absolutely not something you can obtain through

knowledge or by using your intellect. No matter how much you investigate it using logic, the Tao will not reveal itself. For the Tao was not created by knowledge. To truly know the Tao, you must boldly come out of the box of knowledge that surrounds you. You must set aside the knowledge that fills your head in order to purely "feel and experience" the Tao.

That's why, in the *Tao Te Ching*, Lao Tzu said, "The Tao that can be spoken is not the eternal Tao; the name that can be named is not the eternal name." Though you've thoroughly read the *Tao Te Ching* hundreds of times, and although you may think you have "understood" the Tao, unless you feel the Tao directly in your heart, in the very cells of your body, it is difficult to say that you "know" the Tao.

Understanding is very different from knowing. Understanding is a psychological process of perceiving an object through reason. It is, in a sense, conceptualizing an object. But an object cannot be fully comprehended by conceptual understanding alone. Knowing is not thinking artificially or mobilizing rational logic. It is a state in which you come to obviously and plainly *know*, without trying to get it right.

> Don't try to understand the Tao with your intellectual mind only.

For example, understanding an orange conceptually is like reading or hearing a description of the orange's color, texture, aroma, ingredients, and flavor. Conversely, in the instant you directly see and taste an orange, you know the orange. The moment you experience it directly, you know it and there's no need to strain your mind by logically thinking about what an orange is and trying to understand it.

The same is true for the Tao. Don't try to understand the Tao with your intellectual mind only. When you escape from the box of knowledge, the Tao will approach your heart, and in that moment, you will feel it. It's not something you try to force yourself to see or hear, but something you see and hear automatically. That's why, to know the Tao, you must open your "eyes to see" and "ears to hear." When you do that, you automatically see and hear the mystery of life and the cosmos. This is not just about watching or being awed by the mystery of life and the cosmos, but about entering directly into that mystery. So you must open your Tao eyes to know the Tao. Those eyes are not physical. They are the eyes of the mind.

Seeing the Tao can be compared to seeing the reality of the moon. When I was young and looked at the crescent moon, I thought that the moon, round not that long ago, had become very small. I thought the moon got bigger and smaller like a balloon. One of my friends used to say that every night the stars took a little bite out of the moon, which is why it became a crescent.

As we grow up, we come to realize that, although to the naked eye the moon looks as if it is changing its size and shape every day, there is only one unchanging moon. We learn that the moon does not give off its own light, but rather reflects light from the sun, that the shape of the moon appears to change every day depending on the angle of the moon, earth, and sun.

The shape of the moon we see clearly changes daily. That is the phenomenon we see with our eyes. That phenomenon is self-evident and undeniable and appears the same to everyone. We also know that what we see with our eyes is not always the truth. The reality that exists beyond phenomena, and the Source that creates those phenomena—though invisible to our eyes—is the Tao.

The Tao is not clearly visible within phenomena. No matter how much you look at it, the crescent moon is a crescent moon and the full moon is merely a full moon. This is because, although phenomena are definitely visible to our eyes, the reality behind those phenomena is not readily seen. Human beings are great and blessed, however, because we all have Tao eyes capable of seeing the reality beyond phenomena. Seeing the Tao is not about talent or technique. It is a kind of sense waiting to be awakened in all of us.

I wrote this poem over twenty years ago as I thought about those eyes for seeing the Tao.

Everyone has it.
To know what it is,
Take a journey deep within
And open your eyes wide.
Then you will see everything.
Even without knowing why and how,
Everyone has it in one's heart.
Someday, you will see it.
Someday, you will see it.

No matter how good your eyesight, if you don't open your eyes, you will not see anything. So too with the Tao. Everyone has eyes to see the Tao, but opening those eyes is a separate issue. The Tao is there, in that place beyond the limits of rational logic, judgment, ideas, and ego. To see the Tao, we must take away the blindfold of judgment, ideas, and ego that blinds our eyes.

There was a movie in 2010 that swept the world like a whirlwind: *Avatar*. A phrase from the movie, "I see you," became a big hit. "I see you" is an expression used by the people of Pandora, the main background of the movie. It conveys love, gratitude, respect, and a desire to communicate. When the protagonists of *Avatar* said,

"I see you," I realized that they had opened their eyes for seeing the Tao. Jake, the male protagonist who first looked at the world through the lens of judgment and ideas, came to know, as time passed, the truth that existed beyond phenomena and to see and feel the very life—the true nature—of the other person. In the end, he was able to say, "I see you." He opened his Tao eyes, which allowed him to pull aside the curtain of judgment and ideas and view the substance of life.

It's important that we know we have a seeker's heart, the thirst to know the Tao within us, and that we continue to develop this. Next, what's important is to realize that everyone has Tao eyes capable of seeing the essence of things beyond phenomena, and that anyone can open their eyes to see, feel, and know the Tao.

If you have these two realizations, you can now begin your journey toward the Tao.

Why We Must Open Our Tao Eyes

We are already living in the Tao, though we don't know it. Nothing exists without the Tao, for the Tao is the essential design behind all phenomena. Just as a fish cannot imagine an ocean without water, nothing exists in this world without the Tao.

If the Tao is always there, why do we have to open our Tao eyes? Not knowing the Tao doesn't appear to be an obstacle to living our lives. Why do we need to know the Tao?

The first reason is that we earnestly want it. You may want to say, "Really? I do. But I know a lot of people who are not interested in this kind of thing at all." But again, I can say for sure that everybody has a seeker's heart. Though we have plenty of food to eat, a cool car to drive, a nice house to live in, and people we love, we still essentially thirst for the Tao. We all have a thirst to know the something that causes our lives to exist and also grants us a reason to exist, to know some world that will last longer than our finite, individual lives and that is greater than what we see, hear, and feel, a desire to slake the thirst of our souls, which is not satiated by things, no matter how much we have.

The second is that the Tao brings us healthier, happier lives. When we know the Tao that is behind all things in creation, we can learn how to navigate life smoothly, going with its natural flow. Even when waves rise on the ocean of life, we can calm our fears and anxieties and keep our hope and faith in life. We can accept dispassionately the ups and downs of life and obtain true peace of mind. We can go boldly toward the ultimate destination of life, without wandering the vast ocean, not knowing where we should go. We can continue to live more vital, profound, and valuable lives when we know the Tao.

> With Tao eyes, we can accept dispassionately the ups and downs of life and obtain true peace of mind.

The third is that the Tao gives us eyes to see that "everything is one." Those eyes help us move beyond the conflict and confrontation that stem from differences in the perspectives through which we view phenomena. We always talk about phenomena because we are living within phenomena. "I like spring better." "I like summer better." "I like this man better." "I like this woman better." Because each of us has his or her own tastes and ideas, we each view and judge everything differently. The differences in our preferences for, and interpretations of, phenomena create ceaseless confrontation and conflict. In short, we laugh and weep because of phenomena. We fight and are divided because of phenomena. We believe that we are each different and separated from each other. We live our lives divided among ourselves, ceaselessly arguing about what is better or worse than what, or what is right and wrong, because of our belief that we are separate and because of the fixed standards of measurement that we each have.

Naturally, we cannot help having different perspectives if we focus solely on visible phenomena without knowing the substance of things. It's like a child living on the seashore who insists that the sun lives in the ocean, while a child living in the mountains is sure the sun lives in the mountains. Those who know principles, however, know that divisions over right and wrong are meaningless in the face of true reality, and that likes and dislikes are tricks of the mind that change according to our circumstances.

We cannot resolve the problems of phenomena through phenomena alone. We can resolve the problems of phenomena only when we know the Tao, the Source that created phenomena. A perspective capable of viewing all things as one is necessary to transcend confrontation and conflict. This is the reason we must open our Tao eyes, eyes able to view all things—self and other, human and nature—as one. These are all things that through our five senses appear separate, but through Tao eyes, we can see their oneness. The child who lives on the seashore and the child who lives in the mountains will no longer fight if together they welcome the rising sun in a place where both ocean and mountains are visible.

Fable of the Blind Turtle

The fable of the blind turtle appears in the Buddhist scripture, the *Agama Sutra*. The turtle lives in the wide ocean and sticks its head above the water to get relief for its weary body only once every hundred years. One day, when the turtle stuck its head above the water, it encountered a wooden log with a hole in it, floating along the surface of the ocean. Quite by accident, the turtle's head went right into the hole in the log at the moment it lifted its head out of the water. The blind turtle was able to rest very comfortably thanks to that piece of wood.

The Agama Sutra says that our being born as human beings is just as improbable and precious as a blind turtle lifting its head above the water once in a hundred years to accidentally find itself looking inside a log. Being born as a human being is so precious and unlikely, the text tells us, that we should devote ourselves in this life to practicing self-discipline and, in doing so, obtain enlightenment and break the cycle of reincarnation.

> The fable of the blind turtle is a wonderful metaphor for our journey toward the Tao.

I think this fable of the blind turtle is a wonderful metaphor for our journey toward the Tao. That's how difficult it is to become one with the Tao in our lives, lives that surround us with dazzling phenomena that capture our senses on all sides. It's like the probability of a blind turtle waiting a hundred years to stick its head above water and, in that instant, encountering a piece of wood that has been floating on the vast ocean. On top of that, the turtle happens to stick its neck precisely into a hole somewhere on that piece of wood. How unlikely is that to happen? We can infer that the metaphor of the blind turtle is no exaggeration if we think about how few of the countless people who have been in this world so far have truly encountered the Tao.

What's important, though, is that hard and unlikely things can happen! The blind turtle, by sheer luck, did encounter the piece of wood. However, we can encounter the Tao not by luck, but by our own efforts.

The Buddha compared right and wrong, good and evil, happiness and unhappiness in the phenomenological world to mud. And he compared enlightenment blossoming in those phenomena to a lotus flower. We are all born into this world and roll around in the mud, but we are all born with the potential to give rise to a blossoming lotus flower.

In a sense, we are all, without exception, blind turtles swimming in a vast ocean. We diligently flap our four legs about, gasping for breath in the middle of the ocean, not knowing where we are or where we should go.

Do you truly want to open your eyes to the Tao now? The earnest longing to bloom into the flower of the Tao must start to emanate out from our hearts, even as we live fierce, intense lives rolling about in the muck. We must express this, hoping the solid seed of that longing puts down its roots and germinates, sooner or later blooming into a never-withering flower of the Tao.

Confucius expressed his earnest desire to awaken to the Tao this way. "If I attain the Tao in the morning, I can die in the evening without regret."

Feel Ki If You Would Know the Tao

Before, I said that the Tao is the background and motive power of everything existing in the world; in other words, it is the great life force of the universe. That great life force, in essence, is the world of energy. As revealed by modern quantum mechanics, everything in the world is made up of energy, and everything is the action of energy. Since ancient times, in the East, this energy has been called things like *Ki*, *Chi*, and *Prana*, and has been believed to be the motive power that gives birth to all creation, causing it to grow and circulate.

Ki energy is not restricted by the three dimensions of space and time in which we live; dwelling in both the material and non-material, it is like a tightly woven mesh interconnecting all things. In the visible, discernible world, no matter how carefully you consider it, it doesn't make sense to say that all things are one. People are people; trees are trees; water is water. Each of these have their own forms and are separate from each other. Viewed from the perspective of energy, however, people and trees and water, living and nonliving things, spirit and matter are fundamentally made up of energy and are waving in the massive energy field of the cosmos. The power that interconnects the visible world, in which everything appears to exist separately, is the world of Ki energy, the world of the Tao. To put it another way, the Tao is the great life energy of the cosmos actuating all things.

> The Tao is the great life energy of the cosmos actuating all things.

Seeing the Tao, therefore, means knowing the world of Ki energy. It means knowing the principles by which Ki energy operates and, moreover, being able to feel Ki energy and use it in your daily life. That's why I say that learning the ways of Ki is like placing your hand on the knob of the door leading into the world of the Tao. You'll start to see the world of the Tao once you learn Ki.

To learn Ki, all you have to do is feel it. No matter how much knowledge you may have about Ki energy, unless you feel it directly, yours is only half-knowledge. We all have an innate sense for feeling unseen Ki energy. This is a sixth sense, which exists beyond the five senses. All you have to do is awaken that sense. This begins in first feeling the bioenergy flowing in your own body.

If you engage in some meditation, yoga, kigong, or breathing practice, you probably have some experience or understanding of Ki energy. For those readers who have not yet had the opportunity to develop a sense for feeling Ki, I'll introduce an easy and simple method through which you can feel Ki energy.

Sit comfortably in a chair or on the floor, and straighten your lower back. Place your hands on your knees, palms facing upward, and close your eyes. Relax your neck and shoulders and release the tension throughout your body. Calm your mind. Take a deep breath, then slowly exhale. Release any remaining tension out of your body as you exhale.

Now bring your hands slowly in front of your chest. Focus on your hands with your palms together. In your mind, feel your hands with full focus. Immerse yourself in the feeling of your hands, paying attention to even very subtle sensations. Try to feel the temperature of your hands. You get the feeling that your hands are growing warmer. Next, try to feel your pulse. Try to feel the blood vessels in your palms moving with your pulse according to the beating of your heart. Your pulse beats even in the tips of your fingers. Continue to focus on the feelings you sense in your hands.

Now move your hands slightly apart and tap the tips of your fingers together. Do this for about thirty seconds, then slowly move your hands so that your palms face each other with about two inches between them. Try to get the feeling that your hands are hanging in empty space. Imagine energy filling the space between your hands. That energy flows between your hands like fog or clouds. Picture energy filling the space between your hands and shining brightly.

Now, very slowly, repeatedly move your hands a little apart and then back together, alternately expanding and contracting the space between them. Your hands gently push against and then pull away from each other, like a butterfly slowly flapping its wings. Continue repeating this movement until you get a feeling of magnetism between your hands.

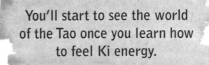

You'll start to see the world of the Tao once you learn how to feel Ki energy.

Try to sense what feelings you get in your hands. You might feel heat or a tingling sense of electricity in your hands, and you might get a feeling of magnetism or volume, as if there is a balloon between your palms. Those feelings arc amplified as you continue to concentrate and pay attention to even subtle sensations.

Now imagine that there is an energy ball between your hands, and very slowly spin that ball with your palms. As you continue to concentrate on the feelings between your hands, touch and spin the energy ball this way and that. The ball is your energy, which is coming from your hands through your concenturation.

Slowly lower your hands onto your knees. Take a deep breath and, exhaling slowly, open your eyes.

What did you feel when you did this? Were you able to feel

Ki in your hands? Do your body and mind now feel more relaxed and more comfortable than before? Your perception of Ki is evidence that your body and mind have relaxed, which allowed your brain waves to slow down enough for you to activate this latent sixth sense. You don't need to be disappointed, though, if you couldn't feel Ki this time. Some people develop their ability to feel Ki easily and others take time. You will clearly be able to feel Ki energy if you focus on this training after relaxing your body and mind and letting go of the tangle of thoughts in your head through stretching or gentle exercise.

Ki energy is a language much truer than ordinary language. With man-made language, you can easily dress up as fact even things that are not factual. Ki energy, however, cannot be falsified. It is life itself. Not even a single flower or small stone can be created through human language and knowledge. Real truth cannot be held in the limited container of written and spoken words. Real truth can only be felt, and it cannot be communicated except through feelings. To convey the meaning of life, you can only show someone a flower and say, "This is a flower." There is no other way to feel the great life force of the universe blooming within the life of that flower.

If you would know the Tao, then start by feeling Ki, the energy of life. When the sense of energy in your body grows and develops, you can feel even the energy of other people, and you are able to watch and continue improving the energy of your own thoughts and actions, and of your relationships with others. You will also be able to read and manage the flow of energy operating behind different social circumstances and in the work you are pursuing.

True communion with nature becomes possible when the energy sense is turned on and heightened. You're moved by the sounds of a bird singing in the morning, and you can feel the principles of nature even in a single leaf falling with its back to the setting sun. You come to realize that you were never alone, that you have always been breathing surrounded by the massive energy of life.

You start to see the unseen world and the world of separate things start to interconnect when you feel Ki energy. This is the world of life energy, the world of the Tao. Tao eyes can see the flow and principles of this invisible energy world. A Tao life is one lived while applying the flow and principles of that energy.

CHAPTER TWO

Realizing the
Reality of Life

IN THE FIRST CHAPTER, WE REALIZED that Tao eyes are not about knowledge or technique; they are a kind of sense we have always had within us, waiting to be awakened. We learned that to open our Tao eyes we must have an inner thirst, a longing to encounter the Tao.

All human beings have a yearning to know the Tao, but most can't feel it because they're distracted by the voice of the ego. In this chapter, we will ask fundamental questions about life in order to awaken our inner thirst for the Tao.

Good questions have great power. When we have questions, answers come to us through many paths and in many forms. Imagina-tion, ideas, thoughts, conversations, newspaper headlines, TV commercials . . . all these things contain messages regarding the questions we have. The best way to find answers to these questions is to listen to our inner voice when we ask them. The most certain answer is the voice we hear from within our being, which we can access through meditation and reflection.

Answers come to us from all directions when our questions are serious and our search for answers is earnest. Good questions can lead to powerful breakthroughs that raise our consciousness to higher levels.

In Zen Buddhism, a teacher will give a disciple a question, called a *Hwadu* or *koan*, as a method for achieving enlightenment. A Hwadu is like a spiritual riddle, a proposition that instills great doubt and struggle in the mind of the student. Serious practitioners of Buddhism achieve great realizations in the process of focusing their entire minds (whether asleep or awake) on solving these puzzles of enlightenment.

In this chapter, we will ask ourselves three such Hwadu: Where does my life come from? What is the meaning of my life? Why am

I living? These questions are probably among the oldest and most often asked in the world. Yet, they are always new, no matter how many people have asked them, and no matter how many people have claimed to have found answers to them. An established, correct answer is nowhere to be found, nor can such an answer be defined in written or spoken words. You must find and experience the answer for yourself.

Where Does Life Come from?

Sitting in a flower bed,
I look at the flower petals.
Where did these beautiful colors come from?
Oh, flowers, beautiful flowers.

These are lines from a favorite song of mine. Whenever I see a blooming flower, I hum the song's melody and feel in awe of the beauty and mystery of life. Where did the colors of these beautiful flowers come from?

If there are any flowers around you right now, look at them closely. If not, just imagine some. Picture any flower you like— roses in glorious full bloom, daffodils awakening from the winter cold to sprout their buds above ground, dandelions greeting you happily on a meadow path. Look carefully at the colors of the petals. Where in the

> Answers come to us from all directions when our questions are serious and our search for answers is earnest.

world did those gorgeous colors come from? How did such beautiful colors come to be in this world?

Close your eyes and imagine that you are strolling through a flowering field in the middle of a beautiful forest. Beautiful flowers of all shapes and colors surround you, emanating life's energy. Listen to the beautiful chorus of songbirds as they sit on flowering branches. Where did the call of those birds come from? What is it that fills their hearts and songs with passion? Where did the green of the trees' fragrant leaves come from?

Now look at yourself. Where did your life come from? Who are you, this person who asks the meaning of life while looking at the beautiful flowers? Have you and the flowers come from the same or different places? Now, slowly raise your hand and touch your body. Touch every part of your body—your face, head, arms, trunk, and legs. Feel the life inside you. The tactile sensations you feel with your hands are transmitted to sensory receptors in your brain. Where did this life come from?

You cannot remember from where or when this life came. It came to you quietly and will leave quietly when the time comes. As a beautiful flower withers and dies, so too will our lives one day return to the place from which they came. When viewed from the universal perspective, the place the flowers came from and the place you came from are not different. Both works of art were created by the universal life force of the Great Cosmos.

We are in the ocean of life. All life is interconnected and is always sharing a place deep within this ocean of life through one life energy. To feel this vast interconnection is to feel the Tao; it is to know the Tao.

What Is the Root of My Life?

Let's approach this question from a biological perspective. Before you were born into this world, you were a fetus in your mother's womb. Even farther back in time, you were a microscopic sperm and egg. This sperm and egg came from your parents. They grew from the food they ate and the air they breathed. In other words, the sperm and egg that gave you life came from natural sources of energy on the earth. These energy sources passed through many stages to become the living organism that sparked your life.

Imagine yourself as a baby who has just seen the light of the world for the first time. What processes did your life go through to grow from a baby to a mature adult? You drank water and milk and took in nutrients from fruits, vegetables, and meats to help your body grow. Countless plants and animals entered your body to nurture you. These plants and animals were nurtured by the soil of Mother Earth. Likewise, Mother Earth is ultimately the one who has given you life and raised you.

> Who are you, this person who asks the meaning of life while looking at the beautiful flowers?

Another essential element of life is the air you breathe. A person can survive for ten days without food, but only five minutes without air. From this perspective, air is more critically necessary for the maintenance of life than food is.

When we perceive only with our five senses, our lives seem to be in our bodies. When viewed with the eye of great wisdom, however, the source of our life is in the air. Just as trees live firmly rooted in the ground, human beings live rooted in the empty air. No matter how healthy our bodies may be, our lives cannot be maintained without the air. Neither plants nor animals can maintain their lives without air.

 Our lives have come from heaven and earth. We breathe in the air from the heavens above and eat the nutrients of the earth through food. Heaven and earth are the cosmic mother and father that support all life on the planet. We are each a blooming flower, rooted in the ground and reaching for the sky. Like the positive and negative poles of a battery connecting to produce brilliant light, heaven and earth join together to make our lives bloom brilliantly. My life is not something I own myself. Heaven and earth created it and are expressing themselves through me.

Those who know that the source of life is heaven and earth realize deep in their hearts the true meaning of the words, "You and I are one." The air that I breathe is the same air that the person next to me breathes. Water that a tomato plant pulled up from the ground only days ago is now in my body. All of life is interconnected as one through heaven and earth.

A good friend of mine described an experience of feeling one with the life of the world:

It was summer. With my mom, I went out into our family vegetable garden to pick some sesame leaves to be a part of lunch. I was snapping off the leaves, when I suddenly saw a cabbage worm the size of my finger sitting on a sesame leaf. The little guy lifted up his tail slightly and was really sticking to the top of that leaf.

Normally, I would pick the leaf the worm was sitting on, and then give the worm to the chickens we raised in our front yard. That day, though, I squatted in our garden, staring at that cabbage worm for a long time.

It felt like an old friend. Without even realizing it, I said to the little guy, "You're trying to stay alive, too! So am I." Without knowing why, I started sobbing hot tears.

Those who know that heaven and earth are the source of life automatically understand how precious they are. Those who don't know this only value the life of physical form and material desires. They readily treat others as if they don't matter. They don't recognize that all life on the planet is connected as one with their own life.

> My life is not something I own myself. Heaven and earth created it and are expressing themselves through me.

Many people go about life meeting their own needs without any regard for others. Those who genuinely know that we are all one naturally show compassion, kindness, and respect for others as well as for the natural world around them. Such people love and protect others' lives as if caring for their own bodies.

Asking after the source of my life,
I realized that its roots are heaven and earth.
Seeking to love myself deeply,
I came to love heaven and earth.

This is the confession and realization of the person whose Tao eyes are open. With this realization, we begin to think seriously about our own existence. We begin to contemplate our lives with greater depth than before. Instead of worrying about how to make a living, we suddenly find ourselves concerned about why we should live at all. In that moment, the seed of thirst for the Tao is sown in the depth of our hearts.

What Is the Meaning of Life?

What is the meaning of life? Before answering this question, take some time to examine your life. Start by writing down some notes about your life as you understand it. Write without hesitation, whatever thoughts come to mind. Don't think too much about them. As you look back on your life's path up to this moment, write whatever is comfortable for you, taking time for gentle reflection.

Your story will probably read something like this: "My name is such and such, and I was born on this day in this place. My parents and family are like this. I have received this kind of education, had various career experiences, and am now doing this kind of work. I have loved these particular people and have married a certain someone. I now have a family with a certain number of children. I have learned these things in life, and what I want to achieve in life is this."

What do you think? As you look back on your life, do you like what you see? Are you satisfied with your life? Are you happy? If you were to grade the life you've lived so far, how many points would you give yourself? Why did you give yourself that score? Does your life seem sufficiently meaningful? Which of the following statements is true for you?

I think life has meaning.
I think life has no meaning.

If you think life has meaning, what is the meaning and value of life as you perceive it? If you think life has no meaning, why do you think this way?

Imagine the following scene: the sun and stars are shining on the earth, and people are living on the planet. You can see one conspicuous person right in the middle. Let's suppose that you are that person.

One day, you were born on this planet. Was the moment of your birth strange and confusing? Your first announcement to the world was a loud, ringing cry. You received a name from your parents and grew up in your own environment to become whom you are today. Few people can say they have no regrets about their lives up to this point. But, looking back, you'll find that you have achieved quite a lot, and that you have loved and been loved by many people.

Imagine now that you are looking down on yourself and how you live from way up in the sky. Seen from this distance, the human form is like a tiny ant. Perhaps you see a person who studies diligently, buried in a pile of books. He studies so much that he sometimes forgets to sleep, and he gets a good degree. Although he has experienced heart-wrenching failure several times, he finally finds his own, long sought-after niche. He works passionately and is successful. As he goes back and forth, busily traveling to-and-fro, he meets a lot of people and diligently gathers things together, like an ant: food, clothing, accessories, books, furniture, houses, works of art. Looking at what he owns with great satisfaction, he mumbles to himself, "Um, this much isn't so bad, but I want more." Those around him look at him with envy. Without even realizing it, he walks with a swagger, and his heart swells with satisfaction.

Are you satisfied with your life? Are you happy? How many points would you give to yourself?

Seen from far away, the life of a single human being isn't much different than that of an ant. We appear for a short while on this planet and then disappear. Everyone dies in the end. From a cosmic perspective, a human being's life and death may not be much more significant than an ant's life and death. Is the universe going to mourn your death more than it will that of an ant?

Let's say that one day you die suddenly and vanish from the planet. What is likely to happen? Will flowers fail to bloom and the sun cease to rise because you're gone? Of course not. Though you've vanished, the earth will keep turning and the sun will rise the next morning. Flowers will bloom, birds will sing, and the world will go on. Your family, friends, and acquaintances will grieve for a while but, over time, they will continue to live their lives just as they did before.

Not a comforting image, but let's go a little further. Suppose that suddenly every single person on the earth vanished—the entire  human race became extinct like the dinosaurs of long ago. What would happen then? What would become of the earth after it lost the human species that once called itself "master"? If the human race vanished, would the earth's other life disappear with it? Of course it wouldn't. The earth might actually feel much relieved, having lost the burden of a trouble-making, headache of a species. The planet's other organisms would continue with the phenomena of life perfectly well, enjoying a well-deserved peace.

If there is not much difference between the life of a human and that of an ant, and if the world would continue to go on fine without the human race, then what is the meaning of our lives? Why have we come to this world?

As harsh as it may sound, in reality life is nothing—"No-Thing"—life is meaningless. Life in this sense refers to "life trapped in the physical body." A life centered in the physical body ends in futility when the body dies. All the material values we pursue remain here when we vanish with the annihilation of our bodies. Without any special effort, our physical bodies grow from childhood, to adulthood, to old age. Our bodies all pass through the same cycle of life, and when we die, we all return to the soil. And it's the same for everyone.

That's why I say a life focused solely on the physical body is meaningless. If we place the standards of our lives only in our bodies, then they become that much more meaningless. This is because, ultimately, we have no choice but to wait for the day when our bodies die.

Dying, in fact, begins the moment we are born. No one is an exception. In the passion of their youth, young people may think that death and illness have nothing to do 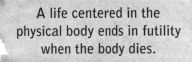 with them. But no one knows who among us will be the first to return our borrowed lives. We are all future corpses. Our physical bodies are like inmates on death row whose date of execution has not yet been set.

A life centered in the physical body ends in futility when the body dies.

Many people live their lives giving reasons to explain why their lives are worthwhile. But at some instant, they collapse when they feel the futility of their lives. For those who find the meaning of their existence only in their bodies, it's difficult to discover the true worth of their lives because the life of the body is not itself eternal. "Life is meaningless." They must thoroughly know this and start again. Attachments develop when they assign primary meaning to a life centered on the body. When attachments develop, they come to have prejudice, and when they have prejudice, they cannot see the whole.

To truly awaken to the Tao, you must realize deep down that a life lived centered on the body is meaningless. The moment you realize a life trapped in the body is impermanent and meaningless is the moment you begin your enlightenment. In that moment, your Tao eyes open—the eyes capable of discovering something beyond the body.

The body is futile. Why then do we live? Have we really come into this world simply to live lives of merely getting by only to die meaningless deaths?

Humans have more than just a body. They have a consciousness that controls and moves the body. But that consciousness is trapped in the shell of the body. Your consciousness, trapped in that very confined space of your body, lacks the room to watch itself. Have you ever had the feeling that your consciousness was trapped in your body and you wanted it to be freed? The way to truly escape from the limitations of the body is to switch from a life centered in the body to a life centered in the consciousness and the soul.

Let's return once more to our picture of the earth. The sun and stars still shine, and biological activity continues on an earth from which the entire human species, including you, has disappeared. Now let's say that one day, after an incomprehensible amount of time has passed, the earth itself reaches the end of its life. Once the earth disappears, what is left? The sun and stars remain. Suppose that the sun also disappears, and that the countless stars in the universe are also all gone. What is left? Probably only empty space remains.

Would you want to exist in such a scenario? If you want to exist, in what form would you like to exist? This is the question I want to ask you.

What exists if the earth vanishes, if the universe disappears? The meaning of your eternal being is contained in the answer to that question. What is that something that clearly exists even when everything in the universe disappears? It is the invisible world of the Tao, not the visible world of phenomena; it is your energy, your consciousness and soul. This is the hope that makes your once-futile, meaningless life truly meaningful and worthwhile.

Why Am I Living?

We are all souls who have come to this planet from the universe. As souls, we leapt from our home in the universe to our home on this planet through the womb of our mother's body. From this safe, dark, nurturing place, we began our life's journey. Often we took off without knowing our final destination, and we tried to find our direction along the way. But sometimes we never quite got our bearings. We wandered along, this way and that, and ended up going in circles. Are you traveling on your life's journey now, or just wandering along?

If you know your destination and how to get there, you can enjoy life's journey. But if you don't know your journey's end, or you know it but don't know how to get there, you will inevitably wander from your path. Do you have a clear landing place? Are you trying to find a way to your end goal, no matter what it takes? Or do you lack awareness of your true purpose and have no desire to search for it?

> Are you traveling on your life's journey now, or just wandering along?

Generally defined, human beings have three kinds of life.

The first kind of human life is physical. *Physical life* refers to all biological activities maintaining the physical body. We have to eat, wear clothes, and sleep, because we have a physical body. In short, the physical life is about the necessities: food, clothing, and shelter.

Food, clothing, and shelter are basic needs of survival. It's only right, therefore, that as born-into-the-world human beings we should use our life energy, at the very least, to a degree that allows us to provide for our own food, clothing, and shelter. These days, however, subject and object seem to have been reversed, so that most of life's energy is consumed by the questions of food, clothing, and shelter. Energy is focused on how we can enjoy a life of high-class food, designer clothing, and luxurious shelter instead of simply eating, wearing clothes, and sleeping.

How can I go to a classier, high-end restaurant and eat the most delicious food? How can I wear more sophisticated clothes and drive a better car? How can I meet a spouse who will love only me and live comfortably in a nice house? For classier food, clothing, and shelter, economic power is needed more than anything else. Those who desire these things have to earn money, so they pour a great deal of time and energy into earning money.

Have human beings, then, really come into the world to experience the nature of a life of high-class food, clothing, and shelter? Do they struggle so much in life simply to eat well, wear good clothes, and live in a nice place? Animals, as well as humans, live physical lives. If humans are really beings different from animals, then there is clearly something more valuable than the physical in a human's life. So what is it?

The second kind of human life is social. *Social life* refers to the efforts spent creating one's value in personal and professional relationships. The value of social life compressed into a single word is "success." In order to achieve success, people study hard, go to good colleges, get jobs, and work hard to achieve something that will enable them to get recognition from others. They have to be noticed in the crowd, so they cannot avoid competition and confrontation with other people.

Social success seems important and meaningful, but it is not a perfect or eternal value. For every successful person, there are always people who have failed. This is because social success is not available to everyone in the world. Success is a limited value that offers benefits to those who have triumphed through competition.

The only meaningful alternative is to pursue growth and completion of the soul instead of only worldly success. Completion is achieved through a life lived conscientiously and diligently toward deep self-improvement. While our usual idea of success is gained only through comparison with others, completion is the process of working toward goals that we ourselves have set for becoming the best person we

> Spiritual life begins with the realization that we are more than just our physical bodies and social reputations.

can imagine ourselves to be. But completion is a value that you can pursue only after you have had an awakening concerning your soul. There is no such thing as completion of the physical body, because it is predestined to end in death.

What we must truly grow and complete is our soul. For this we need the third kind of life: *spiritual life*. Spiritual life begins with the realization that we are spiritual beings, that we are more than just our physical bodies and social reputations. The spiritual life is a life lived according to the Tao.

Physical life, social life, and spiritual life—each of these have value in their own way. Our physical and social lives, however, should not themselves become our goal. They should be means for leading a spiritual life. The body, which is the house where our souls dwell, is an essential and perfect tool that allows us to achieve spiritual completion. It's a problem, though, if these physical and social aspects become the entirety of our lives. The problems of today's world—violence, excessive materialism, corporate corruption—develop because the physical and social aspects of life dominate our collective psyche.

Money and success have become our avowed answers to the questions of existence.

Will you live for your physical body? Will you live for your soul? The choice is yours. No one can force you to make a particular choice. Everyone can discover as much as their own realization allows, and choose as much as their own enlightenment permits. The sooner people realize the limits of the physical life, the more hope there is for everyone. Although there is no completion for the physical body, there is completion for the soul. Growth and completion of the soul: this is the reason we exist.

What Is the Value of My Existence?

The spirit dwelling in your body came to this world because it wanted to experience physical form. Let's suppose it made a contract with its universal guides that there were certain lessons it wanted to learn and certain things it wanted to experience. Ultimately, your life's purpose is to uncover the spiritual lessons that you contracted to learn. You must find that purpose—the goal of your life. No one in this world can do that task for you. It is your mission and your calling.

There are things in this world that are easily achieved, even without much effort. Time flows by and you change automatically, without even trying. Eventually your body fails and you die. On the other hand, there are things you can obtain only with real effort. Finding purpose and value in your life does not happen on its own. You must find this through your own effort.

The life energy of the body can be compared to a battery. Your physical life is over once your battery is depleted. You get no chance to recharge it in this lifetime. How will you use this battery power? When the life energy is used up, will you be free of regrets and satisfied at the moment of death?

How do we tap into our spiritual contracts? How do we access our inner knowing so that we can unveil our soul's true purpose?

Quietly close your eyes and, with one hand over your heart, ask, "What is my life's purpose?" Speak your answer out loud so that you can hear your own voice. Try to feel how your heart responds. What do you feel in your chest? Do you feel the life within you moved by what you said? If you do, then that might be your true purpose as recognized by your soul.

> Answers to fundamental questions about life can only be found within the heart.

Don't be satisfied wtih rational, trite answers. Who you are is not a matter of your material existence. It is not your job, your family role, or your bank balance. Any answer you have to think about is not real. Answers to fundamental questions about life can only be found within the heart. You can't approach them as if you are studying for school. You'll obtain the answer only when you search for it earnestly and with your whole heart.

"What is the purpose of my life?" If you ask yourself this question, and ask again, seriously and earnestly, sooner or later you will hear the voice of your soul. A genuine answer will come to you, breaking through the many walls of the ego that surround you: your name, occupation, personality. You must find an answer that will stand until the time you die, whether it takes a year or a decade. You must get an answer from your soul, an answer that can move your soul deeply. Your soul is the only one who can answer the question. Once you find an answer to the question, your life will start to reorganize itself around that answer.

Our individual lives are trivial compared to infinite time and space. Our bodies, and everything we love and possess throughout our lives, will ultimately disappear. But there is no need to despair over the futility of such a life. Realizing the finite nature of the body and the meaninglessness of a life trapped in the body is an opportunity to open the door to a new, infinite life.

One day, we were given life as a gift. When we accepted this gift, we also received infinite freedom of choice. We can choose who we are and what the purpose of our lives is. We can live according to our choices, and we can even create the meaning of our own lives. We live life in a finite body, but it is wonderful and beautiful that we can choose for ourselves how we will use that life.

There are many paths on which to travel in this world—that of the artist, the educator, the business person, the politician, the religious adherent, and so on. From among those many paths, we can choose the one we want to walk, and we can even create a new path if we so desire. But these are only masks we choose to wear along the way. For all people and at all times, there is ultimately only one path of the Tao. We can walk the path of the Tao only when we hear the voice of our soul and follow it toward growth and completion. Specifics of religion and belief may differ from person to person, but the path of the Tao is always the same. The path that is ultimately unavoidable and must be walked by everyone is the Way of the Tao, and the partner who will be with you to the very end of that path is your soul.

The ultimate destiny for all human beings is to come to know and understand the Tao. We embark on this journey when we come to feel the yearning of our soul. There may be many paths and belief systems that can lead the way, but our destiny is the same—the Way of the Tao. This path is walked by everyone who follows the voice of their soul.

CHAPTER THREE

Recognizing Your Soul and Divinity

IN THE SECOND CHAPTER, WE TALKED about the emptiness and transient nature of life's material existence. We also learned about the power of our choices. Human beings have no choice but to be trapped within the limits of an imperfect physical body while we live. But by choosing a life lived for the growth and completion of the soul, we can transform those limits into infinite blessings.

In this chapter, we will talk about how we can connect with our souls more deeply. As a first step in that direction, we will learn about separating our emotions from our souls. This is because the emotions are one of the most intense reactions of the body and ego, and because it is easy to lose our power to feel the soul and hear its voice when we are driven and controlled by our emotions.

It's difficult for us to imagine a single day without emotional struggles. Several times a day, waves of emotion crash over us. We are happy, then sad; we vent anger, then laugh out loud. As long as we have bodies, we cannot live without emotion.

Romantic feelings are one of the most profound yet complex emotions in personal relationships. When two people are filled with the emotion of love for each other, it can feel like an eternal promise of the soul. When cracks start to appear in that relationship, however, love that seemed as though it would last forever can change in an instant to resentment, jealousy, and hate. At such times, you wonder about the nature of love. To your surprise, you realize that, at some point, many things that once felt as if they were absolute and unchanging inevitably change.

Many people mistake their ever-changing emotions for their soul. And a great many misunderstandings and attachments arise from this misidentification. Your emotions are not your soul. The emotions and the soul are different from the roots up. The emotions are rooted in the body. Emotions arise because we have a body. The soul is rooted in our divine nature. Emotions are connected to the body; the soul is connected to divinity.

Our emotions are bound to change constantly according to the needs and condition of the body because they are rooted in the body. Emotions are like drifting clouds: one passes by, and then a different one appears. Everyone desires to avoid feelings we don't want and to maintain feelings we do want, but emotions are not things we can easily command to appear or disappear with our own will.

What Is the True Nature of Emotion?

Human beings experience emotions because they have bodies. If humans did not have bodies, then they would no longer have emotions. Countless emotions arise in the course of trying to satisfy needs that come from having a body.

The chakras, the human body's energy system, serve as a way to better understand emotions. Chakras are the seven energy centers in our bodies. The first through sixth of those chakras are located along the autonomic nervous system, centered on the spine, and the last, the seventh chakra, is located at the crown of the head. The chakras affect every part of the body by influencing the autonomic nervous system, and are known to play a very important role in managing physical and mental health. Each chakra is reported to be closely associated with a specific endocrine organ, affecting hormone secretion. So when a problem develops in the chakras, it

> Emotions are connected to the body; the soul is connected to divinity.

will have an impact on related hormone secretion. Correcting the energy balance of the chakras is very important because heart rate, respiration, digestion, emotions, psychology, and other aspects of our bodies and minds are changed by hormone secretion. When the seven energy centers are activated and functioning properly, we can live physically, mentally, and spiritually healthy lives.

The chakra system is important because it contains the secret to what we seek: the growth and completion of the soul. To understand the chakra system is to understand the whole of human life, from birth through growth and death, and to understand the system for the completion of the human soul. I'll explain this in detail in Chapter 11.

Viewed energetically, most emotions are closely connected with needs arising in the first, second, and third chakras. The first chakra is located in the perineum and governs needs related to survival and security. The second chakra is located in the lower abdomen, and governs needs related to procreation, sexuality, possession, and domination. The third chakra is located in the solar plexus, and is connected with the need for food and recognition.

Emotions arise when we want to satisfy such needs, and may also arise when we confront obstacles in the process of satisfying those needs. For example, romantic love involves a complex interaction of various needs. Through relationships of this kind, we seek to fulfill the needs of several chakras, including the first chakra's desire for security, the second chakra's desire for reproduction and possession, and the third chakra's desire for recognition. When we are satisfied in these ways, the emotion we call *love* pours over us like a rushing tide. But emotions like anger flare when someone or something gets between us and our object and hinders us from satisfying our needs. Then, when that love is broken and we are left alone, we are surrounded by the emotions of sadness and longing, and, occasionally, by jealousy, resentment, and anger.

Emotions directly impact our body and our energy system. Excessive suppression of emotion, particularly feelings like fear, shame, anger, or sadness, readily exerts a negative influence on our physical and mental health. Most of the diseases afflicting modern people are said to be psychosomatic in nature, caused by psychological factors such as stress, anxiety, depression, anger, and so on.

The energy of negative emotions like anger or sadness first causes blockage of the fourth chakra, which is located in the heart, and prevents the proper flow of energy in the chest. Once blockage develops in the chest, the energy of the whole body stagnates and is unable to circulate properly. As a result, the head grows hotter and the abdomen colder. According to the energy principle in Oriental medicine, the ideal status of energy in the body is a cool head and a warm belly. Continuation of the opposite energy phenomenon, hot head and cold belly, is highly likely to cause a person to suffer from headaches, insomnia, poor digestion, depression, high blood pressure, and various other psychosomatic illnesses.

> Excessive suppression of emotion exerts a negative influence on your physical and mental health.

Changes in our emotions also have an influence on our internal organs. Oriental medicine practitioners believe that specific emotions are linked to specific organs. For example, venting too much anger damages your liver; being too joyful damages your heart; thinking and worrying too much damages your stomach; being too sorrowful damages your lungs; and being too fearful damages your kidneys. Conversely, the state of health of the organs also influences emotion. If your liver is weak, you will be irritable and show a lot of anger. Those with weak hearts often laugh for no reason. Those with weak stomachs are afflicted by worrying and racing thoughts. Those with weak lungs are often depressed and sorrowful over even little things, while those with weak kidneys are fearful and frightened by even small noises.

Emotions influence facial expressions as well as the internal organs. The energy of sadness, fear, and worry often manifests in people's everyday facial expressions. In contrast with this, the faces of people who are positive and overflowing with love are normally bright and comfortable. Just as emotions of resentment and anger have a negative influence on the body, so do emotions of love, joy, and gratitude supply the body with positive energy, healing the effects of negative energy and making the body vigorous and healthy.

Needs and emotions are natural occurrences of life. Emotions sometimes really confuse us because they emerge before rational cognitive mechanisms. You have probably had at least one painful experience caused by a momentary failure to control your anger. Or perhaps you have been confronted by extreme circumstances when body and mind are paralyzed by fear, resulting in an inability to act. Sometimes, sorrow is so deep that it takes away your will to eat or to live.

Become the Master of Your Emotions

Neuroscientists say that emotions occur in the brain. As reactions arising in the limbic system located right under the cerebrum, emotions are the most intense of all mental activity. Emotions themselves are operations of the brain that are essential for human survival. We avoid danger because we feel fear; find a safe environment because we feel anxiety; stand and fight because we feel anger; and take care of others because we feel love.

If we cannot process our emotions, we can become slaves to our minds, which can result in numerous challenges and difficulties. Unconditionally suppressing or ignoring our emotions, however, is also not healthy. Suppressed feelings that are not properly expressed can ruin our relationships and cause physical ailments.

You can begin to master your emotions by acknowledging them in an honest and compassionate manner. As you develop your awareness, you will increase your ability to observe your emotions calmly and objectively, without overreacting.

When we are in pain and overwhelmed by extreme emotions, it's easy to believe that our emotions have a hold on us and won't let go. But actually, we are frequently the ones who do the clinging. We must first realize this to control our feelings: "My feelings aren't holding on to me; I'm actually holding on to them!"

> You begin to master your emotions by acknowledging them in an honest and compassionate manner.

Emotions come and go like clouds drifting across the sky. We do not need to cling to them, as they will inevitably soon change. Yet many people suffer in anguish, clinging to their emotions. They sink their feet deep in sadness, say they are sad, and claim to have no hope as they wallow there in the muck of despair. Clouds of such emotions inevitably hang about longer than others.

There are times in everyone's life when dark clouds gather and rain falls. At such times, people often complain, "When will the rain ever end? When will the darkness lift?" There are others who remain calm, thinking, "This too shall pass." Those people have the presence of mind to laugh without feeling fearful or sad—even when the thunder rolls. Our enlightenment takes root when we calmly observe the ups and downs of life and as we witness the cycle of the seasons, trees growing, blooming, bearing fruit, and withering.

Try to observe your emotional patterns. Do you frequently fluctuate between feeling good and bad whenever your external environment changes? Do you suddenly feel happy when the person next to you praises you, only to feel a surge of anger when criticized? The more severe your emotional ups and downs, the higher the peaks and deeper the troughs of your emotional waves, the more you are being dominated by emotion.

The reason it is hard to escape the domination of our emotions is because we mistakenly believe our emotions are who we are. If we identify with our ego, then we are glad when praised and angry when criticized. Once our anger arises, it eats away at us until we cannot think clearly. But your emotions are not you. Always remind yourself, "My emotions are not *me*, but mine. I can manage and control my emotions because they're mine." To develop this ability, you must become the master of your emotions. For example, when you get angry, you must be able to speak to that emotion as its master and say, "You are the emotion called 'anger.'"

Emotions are like waves rising on the ocean of the mind. Waves are part of the ocean, but not the ocean itself. Even an ocean whose surface is wracked by fierce wind and rain contains great calm in its depths. In the same way, a deep, bright seat of the mind lies beyond our stormy emotions. That mind watches us being angry when we are angry and watches us being sad when we are sad. When we find that seat of the mind, we can watch and master our emotions and not let them lead us about. Our feelings rise and fall like waves moving through peaks and troughs. Let us not be overly joyful, then, when good things happen, for there will soon be times when things are looking down. And don't be overly sorrowful when sad things come your way, for there will also be times when things are looking up.

If our lives are like gardens, then our emotions are like different flowers that bloom and wither year-round, each according to its season. Emotions are very attractive things that occasionally bring dynamic and meaningful changes to our lives. But being helplessly dominated by negative emotions is not a pretty sight. Learn how to live your life by surfing the waves of your emotions instead of floundering about

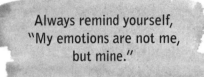
Always remind yourself, "My emotions are not me, but mine."

and going whichever way they take you. Just as it is important to maintain your balance if you want to surf well, you can make use of your emotions freely only when you are solidly rooted and centered in your soul. Use your emotions as a tool for the growth of your soul, as if seated in the ocean depths, watching the waves rising and falling above you with the wind.

How to Control Emotion

If you want to change your emotions, try to change your environment by taking some sort of action. Negative emotions in particular have the ability to drag you into even deeper despair in particular when you hesitate and don't take action. When you acknowledge that the emotions are not you, but yours, and choose to cast off undisired emotions, the power of the feelings associated with each emotion loses its grip. By choosing to take some action, you are mastering the emotion.

When you're angry, don't just simmer. Try changing your location and going for a walk. The energy of fire that has risen to the top of your head will float away on a breeze, and your once-blocked chest will start to open up. When you feel yourself sinking into loneliness, don't just sit there and stew. Try putting on some music and cleaning or dancing. The energy of joy will well up from within your heart, and your whole body will overflow with the vitality of life. You won't know why you are happy; you will just be happy. When you're sad, it's a good idea to stimulate your brain with new information by watching an interesting movie, or make yourself feel better by meeting people you like or giving yourself a reward.

Singing a song is one quick way to escape unpleasant feelings. A new hit song by a famous singer is good, but sometimes getting the words, tune, and rhythm just right can be stressful. So hum the tune without any concern for "getting it right;" just sing without regard for your voice or rhythm. Hum naturally using one sound like "ah," "um," "ye," or "la," which resonate naturally with your energy field. Before you know it, your soul and heart will respond. Close your eyes, smile gently, and sing, focusing on the feeling in your chest. Try to concentrate and sing in a way that will move your soul. The reverberations of the soul spread outward with the sound, and your heart fills with the energy of peace. This is energy you have created yourself; no one brought it to you.

Using activity to manage and create new emotions is just like walking down a new path. It is easy to follow old, familiar patterns, and clearing a new path will take some time. Patterns of emotional reactions are hard to change. Even if you try to react differently, your emotions race along familiar routes. Rather than trying to eliminate old paths, you can build new, even better ones. Old roads vanish naturally into the forest when they are overgrown, and people no longer travel them.

The most effective way to manage negative emotions is to create positive ones. If you're someone who often gets caught up in negative emotions, then you should try to experience things that create positive feelings as often as possible. Emotional reactions can be generated by providing yourself with positive information rather than allowing yourself to passively absorb negative, external stimuli.

Negative emotions cause us to grow more distant from the soul. This is because such feelings usually place priority on individual satisfaction over pursuing the good of the whole. Among the emotions, joy, love, and gratitude are feelings that grow from a connection with the soul and our divinity. Joy, love, and gratitude are the common yearning of all humankind because they are the path to peace. But if joy, love, and gratitude are pursued through the ego's quest for self-satisfaction, they bring disharmony. Such emotions bring peace, though, when they've been pursued for the good of the whole.

> The most effective way to manage negative emotions is to create positive ones.

The power to control emotion comes from the soul. When the soul is weak, the energy of emotion engulfs you like a wave. Conversely, when the energy of the soul is mature, the energy of emotion feels tiny, as if it can't even put up a fight. If unhappy things have happened in your life because you couldn't successfully control your emotions, it was because your soul was weak and immature. If you have been able to wisely govern and make use of your emotions, then your soul has become truly mature.

In order for our souls to control our emotions, there must be proper dialogue between the two. First, the soul must cease to identify itself with the emotions. The soul must seize leadership of the emotions by declaring, "My emotions are not me, but mine!" In the instant the soul makes that proclamation, the emotions will say this to the soul: "You've always listened to what I said. We've been one, you know. Why are you suddenly saying that we're no longer one? You're my friend, aren't you?"

Then the soul must be able to say to the emotions, "That was then, not now. You are emotion; I am soul. You are not me, but mine. I have the power to watch and control you."

Even though you make this declaration, it still won't be easy to be free from the domination of your emotions—at least not at first. As this dialogue between them continues, however, the soul will gain the power to lead the emotions, and the emotions will be tamed by the soul. The soul will recover its central place, its seat as master, and the emotions will act as helpers, assisting in the soul's growth. Once the soul learns to master the emotions, it will come to know that it can also create new emotions.

Why Are We Lonely?

How would you describe the feeling of your soul? It won't be easy to express that feeling in a single word. The feeling is different for everyone, and each of us has our own way of expressing it.

Have you ever had a moment when you felt an indescribable loneliness in your heart? Perhaps you longed for something, but didn't know what? Is that longing? Loneliness? Sadness? Although it's difficult to express in a single word, you have clearly felt some thirst that is not readily quenched. For now, let us call that indescribable feeling the "longing of the soul."

I felt quite of lot of such loneliness when I was young. I was always lonely, whether I was with people or by myself. I would look at my parents when I was in elementary school, and their relationship was so good that they appeared to be unfamiliar with the concept of marital disputes. Still, they seemed so lonely to me. Something about them seemed unhappy and pitiable. I even corrected my own thinking many times, telling myself, "I'm a young child, and my mom and dad are adults; I shouldn't be thinking like this." Whenever I thought of myself, I felt incredibly unhappy, too. I never stopped thinking, "How did I end up here?"

When I was very young, I would go up into the mountains every day and play alone, with no friend to accompany me. When I sat alone on a mountain, I would see energy rising from the mountain in front of me, and I was able to talk with the trees standing next to me. Sitting in a school classroom, though, fantastical things would appear before my eyes as if I were watching a movie, so I could not concentrate on my studies. I gave myself over completely to martial arts in order to forget the loneliness that I could not understand. I felt anxious and strange, as if I'd come to a place I wasn't supposed to be. And that loneliness never went away.

Have you ever had a moment when you felt an indescribable loneliness in your heart?

Strangely, though, if I sat in a public cemetery, my mind found great peace and rest. I calmly sought these places out, even at night, even though other children were too afraid to go alone at any time of day. There, looking up into the nighttime sky, I felt a sense of immense space, and time stood still. Each of the stars in the sky seemed to shine in loneliness, just like me. "Why am I here now?" I wondered as I looked up at the stars. "Who put me here without my permission?"

After ending the wandering of my youth, I finished my college studies, got married, and got a decent job, and my life began to stabilize in many ways. On the outside, everything was flowing along successfully. Every day on my way home from work, however, I would look up at the sky. Overcome by great sadness and incredible loneliness, tears would fill my eyes. I loved my family and loved the work I was doing, but this did not relieve the emptiness and loneliness deep in my heart.

Perhaps you, like me, have felt the longing of your soul. Why are our souls lonely? What are they searching for? So far, I've traveled to places all over the world and met many people, but it has been difficult to find anyone who did not have this same longing. Even people who have money, power, fame, and love—every earthly thing one can desire—complain of loneliness. No matter how many things they own or what wonderful experiences they have had, the loneliness and emptiness of their hearts are not easily filled.

These days, many people choose alcohol, games, sex, drugs, and other distractions to relieve their loneliness. But that is like drinking sugar water when you are thirsty: though you continue to drink, your deepest thirst is not quenched and only grows more severe. When people are caught up in sensual pleasures, they forget their loneliness for a time, but when they open their eyes the next day, the same reality awaits them.

When we are surrounded by people we love and who love us,

we sometimes forget our loneliness for a time. Romantic love, in particular, is the sugar water that is most frequently sought to relieve our loneliness. Human emotions change, however, so these relationships do not satisfy us for long. Even love that seemed as if it would be forever changeless fades and changes with time. Though people we love are at our side, we sometimes still feel the shadow of loneliness.

We seek out other people and poke our heads around here and there, looking for ways to hide our loneliness at least for a time. When that loneliness subsides, we feel happy and at peace. But we are like a duck that, when hunted by an eagle, hides only his head in a thicket for a moment and feels relieved. Our fundamental loneliness still remains there, deep in our hearts.

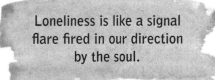

Loneliness is like a signal flare fired in our direction by the soul.

Whether we are young or old, male or female, rich or poor, a beggar on the streets or the president in the White House, we have no way to escape the loneliness. What is the true nature of this loneliness? What can we do for ourselves to relieve the loneliness? Is it like an incurable disease that the human species must accept?

The soul's thirst for completeness manifests as loneliness. Loneliness is like a signal flare fired in our direction by the soul. Our souls shout to us, "Hey! Over here! I'm right here." If you are lonely and don't know why, there is no great need to worry about it. It means you are feeling the thirst of the soul for growth and completion.

What Is the Completion of the Soul?

The soul seeks to move forward toward something. It wants to encounter something and achieve unity with it. The incomplete soul came into this world to wander, earnestly searching for its other half—the divine. Divinity is the light that shines brightly within you.

What is the soul and what is divinity? How are the two different? We feel the loneliness of the soul in our hearts. This means that the energy of our souls exists in our chests. It's why the love of the soul, the joy of the soul, and the sadness of the soul spread out from the chest.

Does the divine nature, then, also exist in the chest? The soul wouldn't be lonely if the divine nature was together in the heart. The energy of divinity is found in the brain. To explain this in terms of the human body's chakra system, the energy of the soul is found in the middle of the chest, the fourth chakra, and the energy of divinity is found in the brain, the sixth chakra.

The soul feels loneliness because it seeks to be completed by encountering its other half, the divine nature. The only way to resolve the soul's loneliness is to encounter its own divine nature.

How can the soul encounter divinity?

First, you must hold within you the dream of encountering divinity—the dream of the soul. The soul has one dream—to become one with its divine nature. To become one with divinity, you must believe in the existence of the divine nature. Your belief must be unwavering, fueled by a sincere desire within your heart. The seed of divine nature slowly starts to sprout in that moment. It is like a mother hen sitting on her eggs, waiting for her chicks to hatch.

Some are moved deeply when they hear the words, "You have

divinity within you," but others listen halfheartedly or with disinterest. These words reach those who have a pure, earnest desire to seek the Tao. A person's divine nature begins to form when a momentary impulse rips like an arrow through the curtain that once hid the soul and embeds itself in the soul's heart.

Free Souls

Second, for a soul to encounter divinity, the soul should be free. In other words, for the soul in the heart (the fourth chakra) to ascend to meet the divinity in the head (the sixth chakra) the soul should be light and free enough.

You may wonder what is meant by *ascending*. The soul and the divine nature exist in an energetic state, although both are invisible. When the energy of the soul becomes sufficiently light, the pure and light energy in the chest spreads out and rises to upper chakras. This is just like the natural principles by which light, moist vapor rises.

> The only way to resolve the soul's loneliness is to encounter its own divine nature.

What then must we do to make the energy of the soul lighter? Let's imagine a basket with a great hot air balloon attached to it. To send that balloon skyward, we must first release the ropes that anchor it to the ground and, to lighten the balloon's load, heavy ballast sandbags inside the basket must be discarded. Now the balloon can rise freely into the sky because the weight within the basket has been reduced.

In the same way, the heart and our egoic mind must let go of the things it clings to. We call the heavy things that hang on the soul *attachments*. They do not actually cling to your soul by their own strength. You are the one holding tightly onto them.

Originally, the free soul is like a colorless, weightless container. The weight of the free soul is zero, but our many memories, emotions, desires, and large quantities of information become attachments that weigh the container down. To lighten the soul, you must let go of your attachments.

If we use the chakra system to examine the reasons we should make our souls light and free, we find that there is a deep connection with the characteristics of the fifth chakra in the throat. The fifth chakra acts as a filter that prevents the stagnant, heavy energy of emotions from rising to the head, opening the way for light energy, purified and clear, to pass. The fifth chakra is the gate through which the energy of the soul in the heart (the fourth chakra) must pass in order to meet the light of divinity in the head (the sixth chakra). If it is to pass, the energy of the soul must be purified so that it is light and free. You have to shake off all the heavy things that are stuck all over your soul. No matter how intriguing or plausible a thing might be, if it entangles your soul and weighs it down, then it is merely a form of attachment and bondage.

If we compare our souls to a scale, then the free soul can be described as a scale that has been calibrated. The scale of the soul must point to zero with no object placed on it. We are all born with a perfect, zeroed scale. As we live our lives and use our scale countless times, however, we lose our calibration. When heavy objects are placed on the scale of the soul, we lose track of it. We cannot properly judge when we are attached to these heavy things, because we can't maintain a clear consciousness. It's just like not being able to detect the flavor of tomatoes in a sauce that is too spicy.

The needles of our scales cannot possibly remain calibrated to zero as we live our lives in this world. There are things that make us angry and things that make us sad, and we are always placing different items on our scales and weighing them. You'd probably have to live alone somewhere, free of all external stimulation, to maintain a zeroed state for your whole life.

Whenever you put an item on your scale, you should immediately take it off again. This way, you can maintain your calibration at zero as you go about your daily life. When you are wallowing in an emotion, you must be able to realize, "I'm normally set to zero, but there is an object on my scale right now," and then quickly set that object down. Just as our scales can rest only when all objects have been removed from them, our souls can find genuine freedom and peace only when they have been liberated from all attachments.

> The free soul understands that everything is a manifestation of the ebb and flow of energy.

Only the free soul can rest in true peace. The free soul merely sees phenomena as phenomena. It looks on all situations and phenomena with equanimity, and without being dominated by them. The free soul knows that everything is a manifestation of the changing ebb and flow of energy. Only the free soul can see the truth of the world from its open, broad perspective, and only it can soar in search of the light of divinity.

CHAPTER FOUR

Three Studies for the Growth of the Soul

IN THE PREVIOUS CHAPTER, I SAID that for the soul to grow we must control our emotions and be liberated from attachments. Once we've done that, the soul becomes lighter, and we can encounter divinity. Now we'll go one step further: What concrete things can each of us do to live for the growth and completion of our souls?

One day, as the result of absolute determination, you find yourself suddenly liberated from your attachments and become able to control your emotions, allowing your soul to grow rapidly. Once you have obtained great realization and enlightenment through several days or several months of concentrated practice, what becomes of your life after that? Can such practice cause your soul to awaken dramatically, eliminating the need for further effort? If your soul encounters the light of divinity, does it mean that you will continue to enjoy that feeling of unity for the rest of your life?

Let's look carefully at what is required to live for the growth and completion of our souls.

To cause our souls to grow, we must first understand clearly what this means. How can the invisible soul grow, and how can we determine whether or not our soul has actually grown? The soul is invisible to the eye. But it can be felt because it exists in the form of energy.

In physical terms, the soul's energy is located in the center of the chest. When your soul energy becomes lighter and is activated, it spreads out from the chest in all directions—to your arms, trunk, and throat. But if your soul has not awakened, its energy remains small and insignificant, like that of a chick that has not hatched from its egg. In this state, you cannot make use of your soul energy, but must rely instead on the energy that comes from the ego, the energy that comes from your emotion.

So what can you do to enable your soul to awaken? Do you wait until you meet a spiritual teacher who can crack the shell of your soul, like a mother hen that pecks at her eggs? It is indeed helpful to follow a guide who knows the ins and outs of the path you travel, especially if she has already completely passed through the process of enlightenment. But if you are not ready to break out of your shell and free your soul, it is useless to have a great teacher beside you.

When a chick hatches from its egg, it pecks at the shell from the inside out. The mother hen, on hearing this sound, helps the chick out by pecking from the outside in. In Zen Buddhism, this is called Jul Tak Dong Gi. In this analogy, the chick trying to break free of its shell is equivalent to the spiritual seeker heading toward enlightenment. The mother hen is the guru who teaches the student the way to enlightenment.

> In order to open your Tao eyes, you must engage in three courses of study.

The chick and its mother peck at the egg at the same time, but it's not the hen that lets the chick out into the world. Ultimately, it is the chick that must emerge from the shell under its own power.

In order to open your Tao eyes, the eyes of the soul, you must engage in three courses of study—that of principle, of practice, and of living. By study, we do not mean the intellectual tasks most commonly associated with school, but rather, we mean the process of obtaining wisdom from your soul and applying it to your every-day life. In terms of energy, it requires the expansion of the energy field of the soul in your chest as you use its energy in your daily life.

Study of Principle

The first curriculum you must master is the Study of Principle. The Study of Principle is, as the name suggests, about studying principles. What do we mean here by "principle"? What principles must we learn?

I present many Tao principles in this book. They are all principles viewed from an energy perspective. The core of our discussion deals with how we can use these principles to activate the energy systems latent within us, live for the growth and completion of the soul, and contribute to the energy field of the whole. Beginning with principles related to the energy system of the human body and the three bodies of human beings, which I will discuss in detail in Chapter 5, they include the universal wisdom and realizations that we can directly discover in our lives and the universe.

You must seek to know the principles that open the eyes of the soul. These principles are universal truths of enlightenment that lead us toward the growth and completion of our souls. Thus, to engage in the Study of Principle is to "realize truth." When you understand these things, you will know who you are, what your essence is, and how you can realize that essence in your life.

Obtaining genuine principles requires more than attaining knowledge. Although invisible, these are the principles of life energy, the source of life, acting within everything in the world, and even within the empty sky. These principles are ones that contain life itself. We must seek a way to activate our life energy, and to use that energy to vitalize the life energy of others. We need living principles that will cause us to shine with the energy that fills all humans and organisms on the planet, as well as the inorganic environment.

These principles were not created by anyone. Nor did someone receive a message and record it in a book. They are the living principles of nature and the cosmos that simply exist as they are. Whether you know them or not, whether people recognize or deny them, whether human beings praise or ignore them, they are the law and truth of life energy, self-existent, without beginning and without end.

One of these principles is the "Principle of Revolution and Rotation." The earth rotates once a day and simultaneously revolves around the sun along with the other planets. What would happen if the earth suddenly decided to go in another direction? What if one day it said, "I'm going to move my own way without orbiting the sun"?

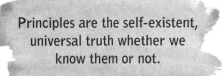

Principles are the self-existent, universal truth whether we know them or not.

By breaking the order of the solar system, she would collide with other planets and satellites, giving rise to unimaginable chaos. The continued survival of the earth cannot be guaranteed without a stable orbit. There is no rotation without revolution.

This principle of nature—Revolution and Rotation—is also reflected in the lives of individuals as well as those of entire communities. Regardless of how great the influence of a single person or organization is, its growth will be limited if that influence does not promote the good of the whole. If it is recognized early that a specific component is moving in the wrong direction, its orbit can be corrected and everything returned to normal. But if this is recognized too late, and it is no longer possible to put it back on track, the direction of movement could destroy not only that individual component, but also the entirety to which it belongs.

This suggests that the destiny of an organization depends on what individuals belonging to that organization do. In the same way, the fate of the earth depends on the actions of the individuals and organizations that belong to that greatest of wholes. The individual component that continues to spin where it is, ceaselessly bringing in energy from the outside to maximize only its own benefit and never pursuing revolution, is like a tissue-destroying cancer cell. The organism that manifests the life principle of the cosmos and nature, Revolution and Rotation, will survive, while the organism that goes against the principle will destroy itself or both itself and the community of which it is a part.

The Principle of Revolution and Rotation is a principle of life at work in all of creation, from the movement of the electrons spinning around an atomic nucleus, to the relationships of individuals and organizations, human beings and the earth, the earth and the solar system, and the solar system and the galaxy. Life is based on the principle of harmony. When we understand this principle, we can discover a point of harmony from which the interests of the individual can be connected naturally with the interests of the whole, and the life energy of the individual can be amplified to contribute to the life energy field of the whole.

So, the Study of Principle is about awakening to the action of invisible life energy in nature and the cosmos, and about realizing that the principles that govern this energy apply to human life as well as to nature. As a part of nature, human beings are not excluded from cosmic principles. They thrive when they adapt themselves to those principles, and are ruined when they try to escape from them.

Studying principles is like looking at a map before setting out on a journey. For example, let's say that you are going to run in a marathon. Before doing the marathon, you put plenty of time into studying the course of the race. You will have to identify in advance important information, such as the topography of the course, where it goes over hills and around turns, where the water stations are set up, the weather, temperature, and wind speed on the day of the race, whether the wind is in your face or at your back, and where the finish line is. Only then will you be able to picture the whole course in your head, avoid losing your bearings, and control your pace.

> Studying principles is like looking at a map before setting out on a journey.

Just as a marathoner controls her pace as she runs by using information she has acquired in advance, we too can make use of the principles we study in advance as we travel the path we walk for the growth of our souls. How can we make use of principles? Principles have three characteristics: those of a mirror, a sword, and a bell.

There is a story in *Sam Kuk Yu Sa* (Memorabilia of the Three Kingdoms) that was written by the Buddhist monk Ilyeon during Korea's Goryeo Period. The character Hwanung appears in this history. He is the son of the Lord of Heaven, Hanin, who rules the Kingdom of Heaven. One day, he has a desire to rule the terrestrial world, and he shares that desire with his father Hanin. Encouraging his son, Hanin hands him three symbolic objects, which he says will help him rule the terrestrial world well. They are a sword, a mirror, and a bell.

Different political and historical interpretations are possible for this sword, mirror, and bell, but I believe they have a spiritual meaning. The sword, mirror, and bell Hanung receives from his father symbolize the spiritual authority and wisdom he should never lose as the son of the Lord of Heaven. I believe that the principles we study have the character of the mirror, sword, and bell of Hanung.

All principles have three main characteristics: those of a mirror, a sword and a bell; in other words, those of reflection, refinement, and realization.

Just as a mirror reflects who you are on the outside, principles reflect who you are on the inside. They are a reflection of your innermost beliefs and are portrayed in your outermost actions. If you have not spent time to clearly define your life principles, this is the first step in the growth of your soul. Go inward and ask your soul: Am I pursuing life based solely on my own individual desires or for the growth of my soul? Do I have compassion for others? Do I consider how my actions affect the world around me? Am I living a life based on truth and benevolence for all?

Upon reflection, if you don't like what you see, you have the ability to refine your principles. Just as our ancestors used stones to sharpen their swords for survival, or remove things in their path, we can use our principles to hone our skills for living. Like a sword, our principles can help us cut away those beliefs or actions that no longer serve us, and point us in a better direction. Principles can help us strip away the illusions of our ego. If we find that our principles are not helping us to create a better self and a better world, we can discard them and carve out new, more benevolent principles by which to live. We can wipe our slate clean like the blade of a sword and begin to carve out a new life.

Once you have refined your principles, you will begin to learn what rings true for you. When you accept and acknowledge a principle as part of you, it reverberates throughout your entire being like a clear bell signaling something new at a specific point in time. When you accept a principle as part of the authentic you, it is often a moment of realization that you are part of a bigger whole. You know what you stand for, and you can go out and share your experiences with the rest of the world. This moment of realization is like opening yourself up to a direct link with the Cosmos.

To escape from our current consciousness and work for the growth of our souls, we must first get our principles straight. Unless our principles are correct, our judgment is clouded and we cannot see the essence of things. We become lost in and distracted by phenomena. If your life is or has been bound to something frustrating and unclear, then it was because you lacked clear principles. Your principles must change first.

> Like a sword, our principles can help us cut away the things that no longer serve us.

The Study of Principle is also like sowing good seeds in the ground. Principle is a kind of seed. There are many varieties of seed. Some seeds produce beautiful flowers and abundant fruits; others produce weeds that compete with desirable plants; still others produce plants that invade the territory of other plants, stealing their nutrients and killing them. Even seeds from the same species vary: some high-quality seeds sprout and produce good growth; others of poor quality either produce negligible growth or completely fail to sprout at all.

What kind of seed would you choose? What principles will germinate and grow into beautiful flowers within your soul? The seeds of true principles will produce beautiful flowers that bring pride to the sower and give the gift of color and fragrance to others.

At its core, studying the principles is simple. It is a matter of knowing that you came into this world not just for your body, but for the growth and completion of your soul. Ultimately, it is about awakening to the life energy given to you and knowing the way of life energy so that you may use as much as possible for the good of all, including yourself.

To truly understand these principles, you must put them into action in your life. It is not enough to simply comprehend them in the intellectual mind. Just as having a lot of knowledge about oranges cannot compare to tasting a single slice of the fruit, having a great deal of knowledge about principle cannot compare to awakening to principle through your body and putting it into action.

After reading books on spiritual topics, many people think, "Now I know all there is to know about human consciousness and the world. I am a spiritual person." Many so-called spiritual people show their enlightenment off like some kind of accessory, when in fact they only have cursory knowledge of what it is.

Enlightenment understood intellectually is merely head knowledge received from another person, not a fruit that you have developed and picked directly from your own body. No matter how great the breadth of your knowledge, it is completely inadequate for awakening to the genuine principles of life unless you feel and realize them through your body. The greatest Study of Principle is awakening to it directly through your body, not simply accepting it in your mind as knowledge that someone has taught you.

Of course, understanding principles through the intellectual mind may be better than not knowing any principles at all. It can be a starting point for deeper understanding. However, intellectual knowledge can easily develop into prejudice and conceal enlightenment concerning genuine truth. Those least likely to become enlightened are people who think they know enlightenment when they do not. There is a big difference between understanding and awakening. Thus, you must look at yourself seriously and acknowledge your blind spots in order to determine whether you truly practice principle or not.

Study of Practice

If the Study of Principle signifies the realization of truth, then the Study of Practice is a process of learning and developing that realization of truth through the body. Many people usually use their bodies to satisfy their own physical desires and emotions, and are unaware that they have within them a perfect system for experiencing the growth and completion of the soul. This system is based on the universal

> The Study of Principle is a process of learning and developing the realizatioin of truth through the body.

life force that permeates all living things—energy (or Ki). This energy system is the same one that forms the basis of all Asian healing and martial arts forms.

In Korean, the Study of Practice is called *Suhaeng*. Su means to cultivate or improve by training; Haeng means to act, do, or move. In other words, Suhaeng is an expression that signifies training movements of the body. Going deeper, it means training the mind by training movements of the body.

What kinds of body movements are required? This phrase refers to all movements of the human body, including looking, listening, speaking, eating, and sleeping. "Movement of the body" actually signifies the daily life of a human being. In its broadest sense, our lives are themselves our practice.

How we deal with the events of our lives is the ultimate form of practice. For example, let's say that someone experiences the death of a parent or sibling when she is young. Such an experience is extremely painful and difficult to accept as reality. The experience shapes her view of life, and she says, "People die like that!" The grief of having lost a family member to death will find a place deep in her heart, but because of this experience, she will anguish even more in search of an answer to the question: "We all die in the end, so what in the world is the real meaning of life?" This person experienced early the final period that comes at the end of life's story.

If she takes the experience as an opportunity for growth, she will realize that the life of the body is not all there is and will seek that something that lies beyond physical life. In the short term, the death of a family member is extremely painful, yet in the long term, that event may cause the bereaved to look into the meaning of life more deeply and may add greater depth to her life.

When something happens, do you laugh and cry, seeing only the phenomena involved? Or do you seek the meaning behind the phenomena, using it as an opportunity for the growth of your soul? The things that happen during our lives, whether we like them or not, are the objects of our study and contribute to our awakening to the transience of life and to the development of our souls.

If the reality you face is painful, then welcome it boldly, without trying to keep it at arm's length. Think as if everything in life, whether sweet or bitter, is ultimately the object for your practice, furthering you in your study. Life is a training ground for enlightenment. Your soul will become stronger and stronger within the patience, forgiveness, and love you learned there.

The Study of Practice is "the process of experiencing principles through the body." Your belief systems, your principles, are embedded in every cell of your body. As you refine your principles, you must consciously work to implant them in your physical being. As your body changes and becomes stronger, more grounded in your principles, your mind also changes and becomes stronger. The Study of Practice requires strength and discipline and helps you develop an unwavering mind. Through practice you develop confidence and conviction in your beliefs.

If the Study of Principles allows you to investigate the lay of the course before you run the race, then the Study of Practice is actually running the marathon itself. It is directly experiencing and confirming with your body the information you've heard in advance: where the hilly sections are, what places are easier and flat, whether the wind is in your face or at your back. You have no power if you have only engaged in the Study of Principle. There is no way for your confidence and power

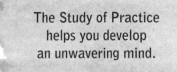

The Study of Practice helps you develop an unwavering mind.

to come alive when you talk of things derived from someone else's experience, not your own. Only a person who has actually run the course on her own two feet can experience it with her whole body, in every cell. Only she really knows how out of breath she was and how much her legs hurt; only she can give you real, detailed information coming out of that experience.

Principles become genuine, living knowledge when you have felt them with your whole body and with every fiber of your being through the Study of Practice. Living knowledge manifests in action naturally and automatically, without calculations or concerns for the opinions of others.

How, then, can we achieve full knowledge through the body?

We carry countless bits of information in our bodies in the

form of habits and memories. There are generally three forms of information. The first is genetic information, which is contained in the DNA we receive from our parents. The second form of information is the knowledge we obtain through our parents, at school, and through books, TV, the Internet, and other media. The third is experiential information: feelings and other data we actually obtain through our own experience. This includes information we obtain through recognized processes as well as information that ends up making a home in our heads without our being aware of it.

An aggregate of such information comprises you, and your actions are controlled by such information. Is this information and knowledge complete, then? Can you say that the knowledge you have is 100 percent complete? It will never be complete. Many people become endless seekers in this way. They fiddle about with this or that and poke their heads in different places to fill a hole inside them. Yet, no matter how hard they search, something always feels lacking.

What is holistic knowledge? How can you discover it? I say that holistic knowledge is to be found within you and you can obtain it through your body. Holistic knowledge is none other than enlightenment you obtain through your own actions, and the process of arriving at that enlightenment is practice.

Practice is essentially a process of emptying. To put it simply, it's about purifying information. Throughout our lives we are subject to billions of bits of information that come to us from various sources. Some of this information is carried in our bodies, in our DNA and cells, based on experiences or memories from the past. Other information is fed to us by outside sources such as our parents, teachers, politicians, religious leaders, TV, books, and the like. Still more is information we gain first-hand through our own experiences.

The information that has entered your consciousness is embedded deep within your cells, controlling your thoughts, emotions, and habits. Practice through the body is a process of filtering out such information. Eventually you recover your pure, original state of mind. In that original, pure state you will know the essence of life itself.

> Practice is essentially a process of emptying. It's about purifying information.

Enlightenment is not something that comes through prayer. Pretending to be enlightened doesn't do any good either. You may put a soybean in front of you, but it won't turn into tofu no matter how much you may pray, "Please turn this soybean into a delicious cake of tofu." If you really want to eat some tofu, you have to grind soybeans. The same goes for the Study of Practice.

Three Methods of the Study of Practice

The Study of Practice can be divided into three general methods: Jigam, Joshik, and Geumchok.

Jigam: Calming Your Mind

The first method of the Study of Practice is *Jigam*. In Korean, Ji means "to stop" and Gam means "feelings" or "sensations." So the word Jigam means to "stop feelings coming from the five senses" or "stop emotions." The name suggests a way to calm the mind, making it clear and still, unperturbed by the waves of emotions. If, for a moment, you close your eyes and listen to what goes on inside, you will see how busy the mind is, how it chatters restlessly. You cannot get rid of this endless stream of thought simply by trying to make it stop. Actually, the more you strive to eliminate it, the louder the noise becomes.

The key to becoming free of noise is to grab hold of the mind's center. Throughout history, people have developed ways to gain control over the mind. For example, yoga cultivates physical and mental balance through fixed positions; koans of Zen Buddhism focus the mind on a single question; and asceticism intentionally applies pain to the body. But such approaches are difficult to endure without considerable powers of concentration and physical conditioning, so they are not easy for ordinary people to use.

That's why I advocate Jigam, an easy method for stopping the emotions. It involves focusing on the feeling of Ki energy that is constantly circulating inside and outside of our bodies. In order to detect this flow of Ki, our brain waves must slow to a rhythmic alpha state. This happens only when our thoughts and emotions have been calmed and quieted.

Jigam begins in the hands because they are especially sensitive to sensation. As you focus on your hands the way you did in the first chapter, you can easily feel the flow of energy, and this allows you to silence your mind. If you continue to repeat this Jigam practice, eventually your entire body will become sensitive to the energy. At some point, an energy center will form in your body, and particularly in your lower abdomen. Your practice will deepen to a point where, without even really trying, the energy center in your abdomen can lay hold of your mind like an anchor. This is when true mind and body training begins.

Many people mistakenly believe that their thoughts and emotions are the essence of who they are. By calming our mind through Jigam practice, we can begin to experience our thoughts and emotions as ephemeral, like waves rising and falling on the ocean of consciousness. There is no need to think, "I have to let go of my thoughts. I have to stop and control my emotions." When you practice Jigam and tune into your energy, your thoughts will simply vanish, your emotions will calm, and you will be able to experience yourself as you really are in the world of energy, the ocean of life.

> Jigam training allows you to go within and experience yourself at your deepest level.

Jigam training allows you to go within and experience yourself at your deepest level. This is the most basic discipline of practice for awakening to the Tao.

Joshik: Controlling Your Breath

The second method of the Study of Practice is *Joshik*. In Korean, Jo means "to control" and Shik means "breathing." Thus, Joshik means to control the breath. By controlling your breathing, you calm your emotions and control your mind. We can understand the patterns of our thoughts and emotions if we examine the patterns of our breathing. We fume when we are angry, huff and puff when we are in a hurry, giggle when we are happy, and let out long sighs when we are sorrowful.

What would your breathing be like if your mind was at rest, completely and utterly peaceful? Your respiration would be so deep, subtle, and comfortable that it would barely even move a feather held beneath your nose. Right now, give yourself one minute of time to enter into such comfortable breathing. You will experience your breathing and your mind growing more comfortable as you let go of more thoughts and emotions with each breath. Along with Jigam, Joshik is a method for controlling the emotions and awakening to the essence of life. By controlling your breathing, you calm the waves of your emotion and return to a peaceful state, a state of pure life.

With the breath, life energy enters and exits our bodies. Consequently, by controlling our breathing, we can control the energy in our bodies. You probably have had the experience of letting out a long exhalation from your mouth, "Hooo…," to calm your mind when you were fuming in anger. And if that wasn't enough, you may have gone out for a walk, exhaling with relief. Exhaling like this for a while will help your mind to settle down as a sensation of heaviness leaves your chest.

By focusing on your breath, you expel pent-up internal energy and bring in fresh external energy. This energy exchange directly affects your body and mind. Through breathing, your energy becomes clearer, and your body and mind become more comfortable. You can even enhance the circulation of energy to increase the temperature of your body by taking in a big breath. Also, by taking long, deep breaths all the way to your lower abdomen, you can store up energy in your body to create a powerful energy center there.

Once you can control your energy through breathing, you can also create your own thoughts and emotions. This means much more than simply maintaining a cool demeanor in the face of difficult emotional situations. Rather, it means that you can literally choose your emotions according to your own purposes. In this way, you can learn how to regulate the flow of energy and the working of your mind by controlling your breathing.

Once we understand the power of breathing, it becomes a simple but very deep form of training. The significance of breathing also becomes greater as we go deeper into practice. If we add the element of devotion, we come to know the deeper significance of respiration. In other words, we come to know the substance of life. Breathing is the most concrete expression of life, and we come to realize that breath ceaselessly flowing in and out with life energy of the cosmos. Breath is the reality of life. When we inhale, body and mind become one, and we are grateful for our bodies; when we exhale, we become one with the air and are grateful to the sky. As we do this, the boundary between inside and outside our bodies disappears; we become breath itself, which is never confined—inside or outside.

> Regulate the flow of energy and the working of your mind by controlling your breathing.

Geumchok: Controlling Your Desires

The third method of the Study of Practice is *Geumchok*. In Korean, Geum, means "to prohibit" and Chok means "to bump against or come into contact with." In other words, Geumchok means to prohibit contact. "Contact" signifies a meeting between external physical stimuli and our body's senses, which form the perceptions of our mind.

External information enters our brains through our sensory receptors: our eyes, ears, nose, tongue and skin. By prohibiting contact, Geumchok keeps external stimuli from encountering our sensory organs. This is because our senses lean solely toward the external when we depend on them. Thus, through Geumchok, we block the introduction of information from the outside. When we limit the amount of information coming in through the five senses, we are better able to access the more subtle receptors of the subconscious realm, often referred to as the sixth sense.

Geumchok practice requires limiting the temptations and

compromises that result from the needs of the body. Because the body always seeks to remain in a comfortable state, it is subject to the voices of the five senses. Eating, sleeping, resting comfortably—these are instinctual needs of the body. Our physical form grumbles and complains when we do not satisfy these needs. Geumchok practitioners close their ears to all the tempting voices calling for compromise when we refuse to listen to what our bodies want. At such times they hear another voice, that of their innermost purpose—the voice of the soul. The path of Geumchok training begins when you decide to choose the voice of the soul over the voice of the flesh.

If you want to understand this more easily, consider some of the diets and workouts. Let's say you have been on a diet that allows only one meal a day and have also been jogging for an hour a day, and that you have done this for one week. How your mouth waters when you see food in that state! You will hear the voice of temptation calling you to dump the diet and eat to your heart's content. What about jogging? You will be attacked by all kinds of temptations from the body: "I'm already hungry, why should I have to run? This is really going to hurt my legs! Couldn't I take a break, just today?" But you will also hear another voice, "No, you must endure! Didn't you decide to diet for two weeks? You're doing well right now. You're already halfway there, aren't you? Let's try a little harder!"

At such times, will you choose the voice that comes from the needs of your body or the voice that comes from inner determination? Closing your ears to the voice of the five senses and listening to the voice of inner will at such a crossroad is Geumchok in practice. Your mind will gradually grow stronger when you repeatedly choose to listen to your inner convictions, and you will be able to overcome the voice of your bodily needs easily. When your will taps into a deeper place inside of you, you will hear the voice of the soul. You come to encounter the essence of life within you when you cease communications with your sensory organs and focus your consciousness wholly on what is within you.

Jesus's forty-day fast in the wilderness and the Buddha's six years of ascetic practice were both similar to practices of Geumchok, designed to help the seeker experience the essence of life. Not everyone has to go to the extremes that Jesus and the Buddha did, though.

I also chose the method of extreme ascetic practice by not eating, lying down, or sleeping for twenty-one days. But I do not recommend this approach for everyone. This method worked for me because I had a strong physical constitution, honed through two hours of daily martial arts practice since childhood. Also, I engaged in the practice when I was thirty years old and in peak physical condition. Even

> The path of Geumchok begins when you decide to choose the voice of the soul.

so, I came close to dying several times during that twenty-one-day period. I could endure the fasting, but not lying down and not sleeping was excruciating, and it presented a powerful temptation that was truly difficult to overcome.

A method of Geumchok you can practice in your daily life is breaking your bad habits. For example, you might overeat or like sweet foods, you might sleep late in the morning, or you might be unable to resist temptations like games, alcohol, or tobacco. Such bad habits accumulate because you continually listen to what your body wants.

Your inner will can develop when you listen to the voice of your soul instead of listening to the voices of those desires. Continuing to develop good habits, like regular exercise or self-development, as well as breaking bad habits, requires an inner will capable of sustaining those efforts, so this can be a good method of Geumchok.

If you practice Geumchok regularly, you will develop patience and perseverance in your everyday life. One training method of practicing Geumchok for this purpose involves gathering and circulating Ki in the body while maintaining a single posture for a specific period of time. Holding that posture is extremely difficult, so it is natural to want to give up before the time expires. Those who give up and choose to answer the grumblings of their bodies are choosing not to grow at that time. Those who choose the convictions of their inner will, completing the specified time without giving up, go beyond the limits of mind and body. If you repeat this process, you develop the power of perseverance in the face of your body's limits.

Both Jigam and Joshik are relatively easy practices compared to Geumchok. Still, you must not favor them because they are easier. It's like being picky, eating only food you like. Being picky about what you eat, if severe, can lead to nutritional imbalance. Only doing easy training like Jigam and Joshik makes it difficult to develop mental and physical strength.

You must train your body to develop strength. Strength does not develop with only easy, gentle exercises. You must learn how to endure and overcome difficulties. Difficult tasks require exertion. When you exert yourself, you increase your inherent capacity to manifest energy. During Geumchok training, when you choose the voice that says, "I can do it!" when it is so hard that you want to give up, new energy strength will surge through you, and your soul will be able to stand in its proper place.

Jigam, Joshik, Geumchok—these three methods, although different in form, have an identical purpose: to stop the thoughts and emotions that stem from the body's desires so that you may encounter your deep inner essence. It's like a spring of crystal-clear water concealed by a bunch of foliage. You may have no idea that a spring lies behind all the leaves, but if you use your hands to gently move them aside and take a look, you'll discover that clear spring water flows eternally.

I will stress it again: the heart of the three practices is "emptying," a cleansing process that involves squelching the voices of emotion and desire. You cannot empty yourself by thinking about it. Do not engage in the artificial effort of trying to realize principles through thought. Turn off the lights of your thinking brain and just feel. If you

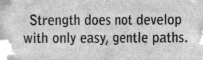

Strength does not develop with only easy, gentle paths.

breathe slowly and imagine you are emptying yourself of everything, the waves of your thoughts, emotions, and desires will start to calm down. The energy in your body will be activated as you continue to breathe, focusing your consciousness inside your body. As the energy system in your body starts to awaken, beginning with the first chakra, energy throughout your body will be purified. Your awareness will deepen to the level of of your unconscious, where an awakening to the Tao will come to you all on its own. When your Study of Practice deepens and your soul commands your body to serve the true purpose of your life, you will begin to gain an understanding of the Tao.

Essence of Practice: Devotion

If the Study of Principle is like sowing seeds, the Study of Practice is like growing seeds. When planted in the fertile soil of rigorous practice, the seeds of principles put down their roots, sprout, and blossom. When the seed first starts to sprout, a weak, delicate leaf comes out, but eventually it grows into a solid, healthy tree. That young seedling does not become a tree in one afternoon. It is a joint project of heaven and earth, created with water and nutrients brought up from the ground and from warm sunshine and air. The tree gives thanks to heaven and earth as it silently makes the most of the life force given it. Creating shade with its luxurious leaves, it provides a sanctuary for birds, squirrels, and people, and produces beautiful flowers when the time is right, comforting the hearts of those who enjoy their colors and fragrance.

We may take a tree for granted, but heaven and earth made generous contributions to that single organism as it sprouted and grew and grew until it bloomed with flowers. And think of how much pain that tree had to endure to grow stronger as it was buffeted by rain and wind. You must show the same kind of intense devotion yourself through devotion to the Study of Practice.

As you begin your morning, do you meditate on your plans for the day? At the end of the day, do you take time to look back on the events that transpired and how you reacted to them? Do you express gratitude for all you experienced? Do you have a training method that you practice daily to clear and restore your energy?

Through acts of devotion and discipline in our outer world, we make our inner world stronger. Practice is the process of implanting in your body the purpose you have established for yourself; it is a time for forming a consensus in your body. In other words, it is for ensuring that your awakening to principle spreads to your entire body and leads to action. It is not easy to remain true to your inner purpose without constant devotion to your Study of Practice. Casual resolutions usually don't last more than a few days, because no consensus was formed between your body and mind, which leaves you powerless to act on their behalf. But inner purpose combined with disciplined practice can last long.

Practice is time just for yourself, when you meet the essence of your life. You meet not the emotions and ego you ordinarily feel, but your essential self, which lies below your emotions and ego.

In Korea, those who show devotion to their bodies and minds in order to encounter their true essence are called Suhaengja. A Suhaengja cultivates a mind devoted to the protection of his or her true nature—the

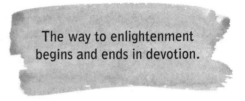

The way to enlightenment begins and ends in devotion.

soul. True devotion of this kind comes from deep within the heart. The energy of devotion accumulates and blooms as something great, and its flowering brings joy to us and also moves the hearts of those who witness our growth.

Many people say that they are lonely and bored. Loneliness cannot fit into the schedule of those who practice spiritual discipline. When they are alone, they practice, and when they are with others, they exchange energy with them. Those who have really learned the ways of Ki are not alone. Heaven and earth are there for them. They are always exchanging energy with heaven and earth, as well as with the many living things around them.

Our souls cannot grow through shallow tricks or shortcuts. Using shallow tricks or shortcuts to obtain something makes a person anxious because the result is gained without devotion. It's like holding on to the skin of an orange while throwing away its flesh. Our souls grow through *devotion*. The way to enlightenment begins and ends in devotion. Beautiful are those people who treat others with devotion, regardless of their status in society. Tasks from which we can learn devotion are always valuable. Those with bright eyes find the Tao in whatever they do.

Devotion is actually something we offer to that which is higher, clearer, and holier than what we experience in a given moment. It is an attitude of mind that yearns to make us more than we are. Those who are strong in their devotion never lose hope in the face of difficult circumstances. Such people always feel gratitude and happiness, regardless of what others may say, or what happens in their external world. This is not to say they don't experience sadness or difficult times, but even in the face of challenge, their hope burns eternal. They are able to recognize the transient nature of life and look toward brighter days with trust and confidence. Also, those with devoted hearts can never be lazy. The lives of those who have lost devotion, however, can easily become a wasteland, and they readily fall into despair. When devotion has disappeared, they become slothful and are easily caught up in complaint and dissatisfaction.

The reason many people cannot show devotion is they do not concentrate completely on the present moment. Devotion is offered in the present. That you are showing devotion is evidence that you are concentrating on this moment now. Unless you focus on the here and now, your mind wanders aimlessly between attachment to the events of the past and worries about the future. When the mind is preoccupied in this way, there is no place for devotion to take hold.

Long ago, practitioners of Zen who wanted to begin their study to obtain enlightenment would not start the practice of sitting meditation right away. Instead they would clean for three years, collect firewood for three years, and cook for another three years. Only after that long period of cleaning, collecting firewood, and cooking had passed were they finally able to begin their studies for enlightenment.

The first three years of cleaning was a time for cultivating the mind. One day, after spending each and every day entirely devoted to sweeping and cleaning, they suddenly realized that they had not been sweeping and cleaning the floor, but sweeping and cleaning their minds.

> Those who are strong in their devotion never lose hope in the face of difficult circumstances.

Once they realized this, they started doing the work of collecting and cutting firewood. At first they would go about this task without thinking at all, but as the years passed, they recognized that the branches they cut from the trees were really the branches of their own chaotic minds. They were trimming the distracting thoughts and illusions from their own distorted minds.

Finally, they would move on to the task of preparing food. Each part of the cooking process required devotion because the resulting flavor, aroma, and appearance of the food depended on whether the cook had been devoted to the task. Too much distraction could ruin the end result. They felt joy when people were happy eating the food they had made with devotion.

In that process, they realized that those nine years, which at first they thought were spent simply doing chores or serving the teacher, were ultimately a time of the teacher's love and care for causing his disciples to grow, and of a practice deeper than any meditation or breathing method. And, in this process, they realize the meaning of devotion.

Although your devotion may initially begin with some ulterior motive, it will eventually grow to become so strong that it overtakes whatever goal you originally had. In this way, when your devotion deepens even more, your ulterior motives vanish, and only your desire to show complete devotion remains. Your devotion itself will become the primary purpose. Simultaneously, your work will take care of itself because you have been so devoted to the present moment. Thus, when you understand the true meaning of devotion, you are finally ready to begin in earnest study for the growth of your soul.

There is a saying in Zen: "Don't share the Dharma with those who lack devotion. Sharing the Dharma with the unprepared will do more harm than good." This is because the Dharma—or principles—offers no help at all for those who want to live a life centered on the body. For obtaining enlightenment, preparation is necessary. That preparation is the attitude that says, "I will make spiritual growth and completion the purpose of my life."

The road to Tao is a life-long practice. You must remain true to it at all times. The morning is a good time, and so is the evening. Try closing your eyes and meditating quietly. "How much did I work today to develop the energy of my soul? How much did I inspire those around me today with the fragrance of my soul?"

The fragrance of your soul will fill your surroundings if you water the flower of your soul through the training of devotion to your body. You will feel great love and pride for yourself, and live amid brilliant light, when you promote the flowering of your soul through daily practice. Your life will be a life lived for the soul. That's why a rich aroma of practice always arises from those who engage in it.

Study of Living

Let's say that someone has learned the principles and realized those principles through practice. What, then, should he do after becoming enlightened? Once you're enlightened, do you need no further effort because, with that alone, everything is perfect? Should you stay on the mountain practicing to maintain your state of enlightenment because, if you go back to your former life, your enlightenment will disappear? And, that aside, how can such a person prove that he is truly enlightened? Is it his meditating quietly in the mountains? Does seeing that make enlightenment conspicuous to others?

No. Though a person claims to have been enlightened, if that enlightenment has no influence on, or substantiation in, reality, then it is not genuine enlightenment. Enlightenment that cannot be communicated is not enlightenment. Genuine enlightenment must not chase after mere ideals; it must be able to sink roots into reality and change reality.

> Enlightenment that cannot be communicated is not enlightenment.

The third study for the growth of the soul is the Study of Living. The Study of Living is the process of practicing and manifesting enlightenment in society. The Study of Living bears fruit when its seeds grow and flower through the Study of Practice. Though it blooms beautifully, a flower that fails to bear fruit is futile. Its value ends when its petals wither, because it has no fruit. In contrast with this, the flower that bears fruit is joyful even though it withers.

The fruit of the soul's growth can be experienced in our everyday lives. Awakening that does not have an impact on reality is like a flower that withers without bearing fruit. To say that it has no fruit is to say that it has no actual influence and that the region reached by the energy field of that enlightenment is trivially small.

Meditating alone in the mountains is not true enlightenment. Some people grow tired of our chaotic world, so they choose to retreat to the mountains and live in solitude. They may call themselves enlightened because they have outwardly let go of attachments. But this form of spiritual solitude is often selfish, escapist behavior. Most of our truly enlightened teachers, from Mother Theresa, to Gandhi, to the Dalai Lama and others, are working tirelessly every day, sharing and interacting with the outer world so that all society can benefit.

If something is genuine enlightenment, then its energy field must flow into the world and among people. Inner enlightenment must be able to change reality as it is expressed outwardly through life. That's why I say that enlightenment that cannot be communicated is not genuine.

The energy field of the soul, located in the heart, grows greater and more intense through interaction with people. For our souls to grow, we need other people to serve as mirrors to reflect the condition of our souls back to us. The most appropriate objects through which we can share with others, giving and receiving soul energy, are people: our colleagues and neighbors, the people of the world. By communicating with people, we can make the energy fields of our souls grow, and we can see and confirm how much our souls have grown.

In the Study of Living, living means just what it suggests: being present in every moment of our day, from when we get up in the morning until we go to bed at night. There is a saying in Korean: "Live the moment now whether you are going or staying, sitting or lying down, speaking or silent, active or still." It means that every moment contains opportunities for the Study of Living.

Getting up early in the morning, giving the gift of a smile to another person, it's all the Study of Living for practicing your enlightenment, that is, principles. That's why a person who has principles creates her own joy and happiness in her life. If you lose your principles, however, you think everything is drudgery—you groan when you have to get up early, and your smiles are forced. The heart of our study is bringing joy to our own souls and to the souls of others through a soul-centered life, a life marked by the fragrance of the soul.

The path toward the growth and completion of your soul can feel long and arduous. In order to travel the road successfully, you must engage in the studies of principle, practice, and living. Focusing on only one or two studies is not enough; you must have the devotion to commit to all three. If you have realized the essence of life through the study of principles and practice, then you must carry these principles into your daily life. Your life will change. If it doesn't, you didn't get your principles straight or you have had inadequate practice. You cannot approach practice with conviction unless you have properly established principles. Also, even though you know principles, if you lack energetic change through the Study of Practice, or are physically weak, the principles will spin around in your head; you won't have the strength to actualize your beliefs in your daily life.

> By communicating with others, we can see how much our souls have grown.

When a change of consciousness comes through the Study of Principles, a change of energy comes through the Study of Practice, and a change of behavior comes through the Study of Living, then it is genuine change. It is, without a doubt, a course of study well and truly done.

Believing in something is not enough to overcome the troubles of these times. We each have no choice but to believe in ourselves and love ourselves. We now need a principle, method, and lifestyle through which we can save ourselves, others, and the world.

Awaken to the principles of life through the Study of Principles, to filling ourselves with the energy of life through the Study of Practice, and to sharing the energy of life through the Study of Living! It is time for us to drive ourselves through the Three Studies for the growth of the soul. Through the Three Studies, let your inner enlightenment change you, and let it flow out into the world.

A long time ago, in the following poem, I wrote down inspiration that flowed out of me when I was meditating, thinking about the meaning of spiritual practice. I want to share it with everyone who understands life to be a process for the growth of the soul.

Journey of Self-Discipline

We have come
To train
Upon the training grounds
Of the world.

Patience, forgiveness, and love
Paths to awareness
God's gifts to all
Provided in this environment.

Body, personality, relationships

Environment and time
All tasks given to me
Are given out of love.

A tree does not complain
That the earth is too dry or too rough
That the rains do not come often
With patience, forgiveness and harmony
It does its best . . . fulfilling its mission.

The mountain is sacred
It does not differentiate
Nor discriminate
Whatever the tree may be
Whenever the rains may come
Wherever lightening may strike
However the wind may blow
Welcoming all
Embracing all.

CHAPTER FIVE
The Three Bodies

HOW MANY BODIES DO YOU HAVE? To this seemingly silly question, you will probably answer, "One." It is obvious that you do not have more than one physical body. Even if you had a twin with a similar body, it would be his or her body, not yours. But I would like to suggest that you have three bodies, not one, which may seem like a strange idea at first.

There is only one body that is visible to the physical eye—the body that you can touch with your hands. It is the one that you feed, clothe, and take care of every day. Where, then, are the other two bodies, and how can you sense them? These two other bodies are found in a world invisible to the naked eye.

Do you have something other than your physical body that you call "me"? Imagine yourself as you were the moment you were born, declaring your arrival with a great, resounding cry. Did you have something else then, besides your body?

At the instant that you were born, you had a body and you had energy, which made that body move. You had consciousness, which watched all of this as it was happening. Energy and consciousness are the other two "bodies" that make up who you are, along with your physical body.

In that sense, every human being has three bodies: the physical body, the energy body, and the spiritual body. These three bodies do not exist in complete separation from each other. The being that is you consists of energy and consciousness combined with the matter of your physical body. These three bodies are each different forms of energy. In short, whether we're talking about the physical body, the energy body, or the spiritual body, they are each made up of energy; these are divided according to the nature of that energy.

Let's use an example to illustrate this. Imagine a glass containing muddy water. When you first look at the muddy water, it appears to be a single, undifferentiated material. Over time, however, the soil gradually sinks to the bottom, and the clear water gathers at the top. Now, the muddy water has separated into two forms—water and soil. But, if you stir the contents of the glass together, they will again take on the form of muddy water.

This analogy also applies to the three human bodies. Each of the different bodies is made up of energy, but this energy takes on a different form according to its density. Heavy, dense energy becomes our physical body, like the soil that sank to the bottom of the glass, while lighter, finer energy becomes our spiritual body, similar to the water that rose to the top. Energy also exists as a bridge connecting the physical and spiritual bodies. Although each of these three bodies appears to be different, they are fundamentally one. Each merely takes on a different form according to its density and vibration.

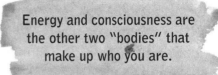
Energy and consciousness are the other two "bodies" that make up who you are.

Physical Body

First, let's look at the physical body, which is the easiest to understand. The physical body is a form of energy that exists in a corporeal state. A flow of energy is essential to maintaining and managing the physical body. For everything in the world is made up of energy, and all things depend on the action of energy. What kind of energy creates and maintains your visible, physical body?

What was the first energy that formed your physical body? In other words, from whom did you receive your physical body? You got it from your parents. Your body began with an encounter between a sperm and an egg, and it fed on the energy resources supplied by your mother's body as you lived for nine months in her womb. When you were in your mother's womb, your skin, bones, organs, brain—all of it—were a part of your mother's body. Your life was sustained by the energy supplied by your mother through

your umbilical cord. Such energy in Korean is called *Wonki*, which means "primal energy." It refers to the energy you have had since the time you were born; in other words, to the energy you inherited from your parents.

As a newly born, independent organism, you got your supply of energy from the outside. At first, you drank your mother's milk, or infant formula, and once you had grown a little more, you ate other foods. You digested food, converted it into energy, and sent its nutrients throughout your body.

But your energy is not maintained simply by eating food in this way. Another important component is respiration. Oxygen is essential for converting nutrients from the food we eat into the energy we need for our body's vital functions. As we breathe, oxygen is supplied to the whole body through the blood vessels, and food is changed into energy through metabolism. The energy we obtain through eating and breathing is called *Jungki*, or vital energy, in Korean.

We can get an idea of the meaning of Jungki if we look at the Chinese character for *Jung* (精). On the left side of this composite character is the character for *rice, mi* (米), which means "food;" on the right side is the character for *blue, chung* (青), which signifies the air. Food and air unite to generate vital energy, which grows your physical body and maintains your life.

In addition to the primal and vital energies that form the human body, there is another type of energy. In Korean it is called *Jinki*, or authentic energy. In contrast with primal energy and vital energy, which are not dependent on mental concentration, Jinki is an energy you can obtain through the concentration of your consciousness.

Do you remember the energy-sensitized training that you experienced in the first chapter? The warmth, electrical vibrations, and magnetic sensations that you felt during that training are phenomena of Jinki generated in your hands. You concentrated your mind on the Jungki that existed in your body, and it changed into Jinki, energy of a finer level.

Mental concentration is essential to feeling energy in your hands. It's difficult to feel Jinki if you're stuck in other thoughts or emotions while you're doing training for feeling energy. Jinki is an operation of the mind that gathers where the mind focuses. This is an important principle of energy training, called *Shim Ki Hyul Jung*, which

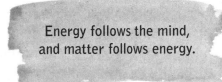

Energy follows the mind, and matter follows energy.

means "where the mind goes, there Jinki gathers; and where Jinki gathers, the blood and Jungki follow." In other words, energy follows the mind, and matter follows energy.

The principle of Shim Ki Hyul Jung is important both to the interaction of the three elements of the human body, energy, and mind, and to the creation and evolution of everything in the universe. In other words, energy is moved by the action of mind or consciousness, and matter is formed by the action of that energy. Ultimately, we achieve creation by making up our minds and concentrating on that mindset. To make up your mind is to have drawn a picture in the unseen world of consciousness. By continuing to use your energy on what you envision in your mind, you move it from the world of consciousness to the world of phenomena. That is the process of creation.

The principle of Shim Ki Hyul Jung can be compared to focusing light through a magnifying glass. The sunlight scatters if you move the magnifying glass around. However, if you hold the lens still and focus it carefully, the light becomes strong enough to start a fire. The action of our consciousness is like this. Likewise, a diffused and scattered mind has weak energy, while a mind focused in one direction produces powerful energy.

In the same way that a magnifying glass converts the energy of light into the energy of fire, our minds can convert vital energy into Jinki. Through the mind, we can absorb energy from the universe, and then control that energy for specific outcomes such as healing and achieving your desired goals. Once we reach a high level of training, we can send energy to any part of our body and send good energy to others. Those who have mastered the principles of energy can change their surrounding circumstances, as well as their own bodies.

I address the actions of the mind and energy based on quantum physics in depth in my book and documentary film, *Change*. The Law of Attraction, which has been discussed in many books, is also the same as the principle of Shim Ki Hyul Jung. Energy collects where the mind is concentrated. So everything depends on what we choose.

How, then, does Jinki help us? Jungki is created when we eat and breathe well, so isn't that enough? There is no problem with using just Jungki to maintain the life of the body. Adding Jinki, however, will provide much greater benefits for maintaining the health and vitality of the body. The really important reason we generate and accumulate Jinki through meditation, kigong, and breathing is that Jinki plays a very pivotal role in the growth and completion of the soul.

There is a specific part of our body where Ki is manifested and distributed. It is the same area of the lower abdomen that most Asian healing traditions and martial arts forms commonly associate with our "power center" or *dan tien*. In Korean, this area is called *Dahnjon*. *Dahn* means Jinki or "authentic energy," and *Jon* means "field." In other words, Dahnjon means "the field where our Jinki gathers." To put it simply, it is an energy center similar to a chakra. The Dahnjon does not exist in our bodies on a material level the way our internal organs do. Instead, it is part of a system that exists in the energetic dimension.

> Those who have mastered the priciples of energy can change their circumstances, as well as their own bodies.

Our bodies have three Dahnjon centers. They are the lower Dahnjon, located in the lower abdomen; the middle Dahnjon, located in the chest; and the upper Dahnjon, located in the head.

The energies in the three Dahnjon centers each have their own unique properties, and each type of energy has a different name. *Jung* is the name of the energy of the lower Dahnjon; *Ki* is the energy of the middle Dahnjon; *Shin* is the energy of the upper Dahnjon. These three energy centers are matched with the three kinds of bodies. The energy of the lower Dahnjon is connected with the physical body, the energy of the middle Dahnjon is connected with the energy body, and the energy of the upper Dahnjon is connected with the spiritual body.

The Jung energy in the lower Dahnjon, which influences the strength and vitality of the physical body, supplies vital force to the whole body through breathing and the consumption of food. This Jung energy can be changed into a form of Jinki through energy breathing that involves work deep into the abdomen. The lower Dahnjon is centered in the abdomen at a point about two inches below the navel and in the center of the body. This place is also the core of our physical strength, and corresponds to the center point of the body when viewed overall. Consequently, the state of Jung energy in the lower Dahnjon is closely connected with the condition of the physical body.

Jung energy's degree of activation is determined by "density," and by the degree of energy fullness. Jung energy tends to become concentrated and condensed toward the center. If you're full of Jung energy, it means you have a lot of concentrated energy in your lower abdomen, and when your Jung energy is sparse, it means that you have little energy and that your energy-condensing power is weak. Jung is also measured using temperature. The more charged you are with Jung energy, the higher the core temperature of your lower abdomen will be.

If Jung energy is dense, then a powerful core develops, resulting in smooth circulation of energy throughout the body, which increases physical vitality and produces a higher level of immunity to disease. In contrast, a lack of Jung energy causes the core to be weak, which inhibits the flow of energy throughout the body and decreases vitality. That's why the first goal of people who train Jinki is strengthening their lower Dahnjon to create a state of dense Jung energy. In Korean this is called *Jungchoong*, which means "Jung energy is full" in the lower Dahnjon. Jungchoong is the key to the health of the physical body.

Energy Body

The physical body is encased by a lighter, largely invisible energy body. The energy body can be seen and felt by some people who have a more developed sensitivity to energy fields. When people talk about seeing other people's auras, they are referring to the energy body.

The energy body exists both inside and outside the physical body. Generally, it extends outward to about three feet surrounding the body. The energy body, in scientific terms, is the bioelectromagnetic field. It is malleable in shape and size, expanding and shrinking according to the extent of a person's energy activation and mental energy. You can often sense a person's energy field, even though

> The energy body is directly reflective of a person's mental and spiritual state.

you may not be able to see it. The energy body is usually directly reflective of a person's mental and spiritual state. For example, if someone walks into the room angry, you can probably sense it, even if they give no visual clues. You can sense this energy because your energy body is affected by those of the people around you.

When I practiced meditation training at dawn every morning for a hundred days, I could see a form in the shape of a person, shining with a golden light before my eyes. Later I realized that this golden capsule was my energy body. When the energy body is activated, it often takes on a clear, bright, golden hue.

The association of the energy body with the middle Dahnjon, which is located in the very center of the chest, is strong. The name of the energy of the middle Dahnjon is Ki. Ki energy's degree of activation is determined by its "clarity or maturity." The clarity of Ki energy affects the size of the energy body. Clear energy can radiate widely into its surroundings, while cloudy energy, unable to radiate outward, stagnates and blocks the flow of energy in the chest. If your chest energy is heavy, it impedes the flow of energy throughout your entire body.

What factors make Ki clear or cloudy? The clarity of your Ki is directly related to your state of mind. When the mind is open and positive, the energy body is activated as well. When we feel love and joy, we commonly say that our hearts "overflow." The expression, "overflow," indicates that the Ki energy of the middle Dahnjon is spreading. On the other hand, when we are frustrated or unhappy, our minds are often closed and more negative, blocking the flow of our Ki.

When Ki energy is activated, the energy field of the middle Dahnjon expands, causing the energy of real love to flow automatically to other people. This is not the joy behind forced smiles or the love that is given out of obligation, but real, unconditional love—love without constraints, restraints, or expectations. It is said to be the love of the soul, not the love of the emotions. The Ki energy of the middle Dahnjon is a fountain of never-ending love and joy.

Those who lack energy in their middle Dahnjon often try to get energy from others in an attempt to relieve the emptiness they feel in their own hearts. They may also try to get it through food or various forms of entertainment. You must be able to regulate negative thoughts, emotions, and stress to manage the energy of your middle Dahnjon well. Negative attitudes give rise to negative energy, and that stagnates the flow of energy in the chest. Stagnation of energy in the chest leads to an obstruction of energy flow throughout the body, which also causes various diseases in the nervous and circulatory systems.

In contrast with this, the more Ki energy is activated in the middle Dahnjon, the less you need and the less attached you are to external energy. You actually over-flow with positive energy, which you end up sharing with those around you. That's why, when the Ki energy of the middle Dahnjon is activated, personal relationships with others and emotional give-and-take are improved. This condition is called *Kijang* in Korean, which means "Ki matures."

> The Ki energy in your heart is a foundation of never-ending love and joy.

Spiritual Body

The physical body is clearly visible to our eyes, and the energy body can be felt through the energy sense. What about the spiritual body, though? Is it difficult to sense?

No. It's very easy. Close your eyes right now, and try to imagine yourself eating a delicious bowl of ice cream. This is probably easy for anyone to do. When you imagined that, didn't a picture come to your mind like an image on a movie screen? You can't touch that image with your hands, but it clearly existed, and you were able to feel and perceive it. Although it isn't visible to your physical eyes, there is a world of consciousness that your brain detects and creates; that is the spiritual body.

The center point of the spiritual body is the upper Dahnjon, in other words, the brain. It is located at a place inward from a point in the middle of the forehead called the "third eye."

The name of the energy of the upper Dahnjon is Shin, meaning divinity. Shin energy is indigo in color. Shin energy's degree of activation is determined by its "brightness." To put it another way, Shin energy appears as brightness of consciousness.

We commonly use brightness to express the quality of a person's consciousness, saying, "Her consciousness is bright," or "His consciousness is dark." This is not just a metaphor. The brightness of consciousness is a real, concrete phenomenon that occurs as a result of Shin energy in the upper Dahnjon.

What is bright consciousness and what is dark consciousness? First, let us list forms of dark consciousness. If we only imagine things like sadness, anger, fear, powerlessness, shame, and guilt, our minds grow dark and heavy. Considering these, it is easy to determine what kinds of bright consciousness there are. Things like love, joy, happiness, courage, forgiveness, harmony, and peace bring smiles to our faces and make us feel better.

Let's look at an example. Suppose you turn on a one-watt light bulb in a dark room. What would you see? Virtually nothing would be visible; turning on the light would do no good at all. You would have to feel your way around in the dark, recognize objects by touch, and you couldn't move freely for fear of tripping over something, so the radius of your activity would inevitably be small.

Next you turn on a thirty-watt light bulb. Now what would you see? The once-dark room would now be fairly bright. Furniture and objects would appear before your eyes, but the room wouldn't be completely bright as if it were daylight. You wouldn't see dust in dim corners, and small text wouldn't be clearly visible, so reading would be frustrating.

This time you turn on a thousand-watt light bulb. The inside of the room becomes as bright as day, making you feel brighter and more cheerful. Because everything is clearly visible, you no longer need to feel your way around, nor are you frustrated over the poor legibility of small text.

The brightness of consciousness is like this. When consciousness becomes bright, as when a thousand-watt light bulb is turned on, we automatically come to see and know the principles of life and the world to the extent that our illumination allows, even without any particular effort. Worrying about and discriminating between right and wrong is no longer needed, because we know the principles of the world, and we come to face ourselves, others, and the world with understanding and tolerance. Our consciousness grows brighter, giving us eyes to see the principles of the world, the principles of the Tao.

> When our spiritual body is activated and our consciousness brightens, we just see and know.

In contrast with this, no matter how much we try, when our consciousness is dark, like a low-wattage light bulb, we cannot properly see the principles of life and the world. In that darkness, we believe that what we've seen is all there is, and we ignore or choose not to recognize opinions different from our own. We live trapped in that dark consciousness, fumbling about as we try, based on our own limited standards, to distinguish and judge between right and wrong.

When our spiritual body is activated and our consciousness brightens, we just see and know. That's why we don't need to believe anything. When you know and feel something directly, that becomes enough. With the brightening of Shin energy in your upper Dahnjon, you come to feel the substance of life interconnected with all things. Perhaps that's why in English, this illuminated state is called *enlightenment*. When Shin energy has reached its maximum brilliance, it is called *Shinmyung* in Korean, which means "Shin is illuminated" in your upper Dahnjon.

The Evolution of Energy

The human energy system develops and is completed in stages. When Jung fills the lower Dahnjon, Ki matures in the middle Dahnjon, and then Shin is illuminated. This principle is called *Jungchoong Kijang Shinmyung*. Jung, Ki, and Shin each have their own characteristics and roles, but they are an inseparable, single form of energy. Jung becomes the basis of Ki, and Ki becomes the basis of Shin.

Let's look at the process of Jungchoong Kijang Shinmyung step by step.

Healthy nutrition and suitable exercise are necessary for training Jung. And there's one more thing that should be added here: energy breathing. Here is how you do it. Breathe naturally with the flow of energy rather than inhaling too deeply or holding your breath. As you inhale slowly, feel the energy, push your belly outward, and imagine energy gathering in your lower Dahnjon. When you exhale, pull your lower abdomen inward toward your back and, concentrating on your lower Dahnjon, imagine the Jung energy there increasing in density. It's important to devotedly take one breath at a time through the concentration of your awareness. When you do that, Jung energy will accumulate in your lower Dahnjon.

The Jung energy that has filled your lower Dahnjon rises along your spine to your chest, where it activates the energy system of your middle Dahnjon. The Ki energy of your middle Dahnjon being activated means that the energy of your chest is clear and mature. It grows even more when it spreads beyond you to the people around you through the energy of pure love and joy coming from the soul in your heart. Clear, pure soul energy rises to your brain, to your upper Dahnjon, to awaken your Shin energy. When the energy system of your upper Dahnjon is activated, you reach a state in which your Shin is illuminated—Shinmyung.

Our physical body, energy body, and spiritual body can grow in a balanced, harmonious way through the step-by-step development of Jungchoong, Kijang, and Shinmyung. To experience and realize this, it's most important to develop a sense of feeling and using energy. Energy is the medium that interconnects the three bodies and is, at the same time, a wonderful tool for developing all of them.

We can feel and know through energy the subtle textures of life that we have failed to detect through words and intellectual knowledge. Energy is the seen and unseen world, matter and spirit, and the bridge that allows communication between them and connects them with each other. Making the physical, energy, and spiritual bodies healthy and harmonious through the Study of Principles, Study of Practice, and Study of Living is the key to the Tao life.

CHAPTER SIX
The Five Issues of Life

EVERYONE WORRIES ABOUT various problems in their personal lives, but there are certain issues that everyone must resolve to facilitate the growth of their soul. These five basic issues are health, sexuality, money, fame, and death. We live our lives tossing and turning, laughing and crying, hurting and being hurt in our quest to solve these five issues. Which of these five do you worry about most? Which do you want to resolve first? How can we be sure when these issues are resolved? These are all formidable issues.

Can we solve the problem of health simply by creating a perfectly healthy body? If our sexual needs are met, have we solved the issue of sexuality? If we become rich, will we no longer worry about money? If our names are widely known to the world, is the issue of fame resolved? Can we drink from the fountain of youth to solve the problem of death?

Most people choose to solve their problems by fulfilling their needs to the highest possible level. But this approach only stirs up competition and greed as people grasp for more and more to satisfy their unquenchable desires. The rich man can never have enough money; the body is never strong enough; sexual desires are never fully met; and so on.

Should we go in the opposite direction then, endlessly suppressing our needs and ignoring these issues? This might work if you live your entire life pursuing enlightenment in a mountain temple. But it is impossible to ignore these issues while living among others in a material world.

"Solving" these issues is really a matter of how you relate to them. First, you must not be attached to them. Second, you must not be dominated or controlled by them. Third, you must master these areas of your life so that you can manage and utilize them for your greatest potential. Ultimately, this means that you must become free of anything that causes your consciousness to be constricted in relation to these five issues.

It is important to understand that these five issues are nothing more than phenomena. If you seek to resolve phenomenal issues using phenomena, you will just sink deeper and deeper into a difficult-to-escape labyrinth. Only *principles* can resolve the problems of phenomena.

To find solutions, you must first know what the roots of those problems are. Health, sexuality, money, fame, and death—the five issues of life—are deeply rooted in human needs. Physical needs arise because human beings have bodies. We must understand our needs and resolve those needs wisely. It is not possible to ignore or suppress the five basic needs of life. They nag us constantly in the backs of our minds.

> Humans have the power to control their desires without being slaves to them.

Through the development of our awareness and consciousness, however, we can gain control over these voices and not be driven and dominated by them. Humans naturally have desires for those needs, but at the same time, they have the power to control their desires without being slaves to them. The way to resolve these five issues is to examine them from the perspective of the growth of the soul and to know how to control and use these needs in service of the soul's growth.

Do you want to resolve the five issues of life—health, sexuality, money, fame, and death? If so, you must first become absolutely honest. You must be able to look clearly and honestly at how these issues are entangled in your mind and how they affect your overall physical, mental and spiritual condition. You need to observe whether, consciously or not, you are avoiding these issues, or whether you are ensnared by them, devoting all your time and energy trying to satisfy them. Let's examine these issues more closely.

Health

Do you think that you are healthy or unhealthy? Why do you think that way? What do you think health means, and what are your standards for health?

Do you think that you are healthy because your body is free of disease? Do you think that you are unhealthy because you are in physical pain or discomfort? If you are an older person, do you think that you are unhealthy because your body is not as it was when you were young? What actually is the true meaning of "health?"

According to the World Health Organization (WHO), "Health is a state of complete physical, mental, and social well-being and not merely the absence of disease or infirmity." Still, most people think that unless they are showing symptoms of some kind of disease, they are healthy. Today, many health professionals recognize that you can be physically healthy, but still suffer from a mental or spiritual malady. You can be emotionally and spiritually healthy and still show signs of physical suffering or even terminal illness. Physical health is the starting point in the journey toward well-being, but not its totality.

The WHO states that, particularly in developed countries, there are 450 million people with mental disabilities. Depression has been recognized as being the greatest burden we will face with respect to human health in the next 20 years. A joint study by the WHO and Harvard University warned that, in the near term, heart disease, traffic accidents, and depression are the three greatest health conditions afflicting humanity. Further, the link between mind-body health is increasingly being recognized by scientists and medical professionals.

In the last chapter, we learned that we are made up of three bodies—a physical body, an energy body, and a spiritual body. The health of each of these three bodies strongly influences the others. If a problem develops in any one of these three, it impacts the others. All three of these bodies must be balanced and in optimal condition if we are to say that we are truly healthy.

If we consider that most of the diseases that afflict modern people are psychosomatic in nature, we can easily grasp the importance of the energy and spiritual bodies for physical well-being.

Health in its physical sense usually means having no disease or dysfunction. Physical health, defined in a more active way, means a state in which you can fully utilize your body's functions and energy the way you intend. This means that you must master the use of your body, becoming able to use it as you see fit, rather than being dominated by your body. Does this mean that those with physical disabilities, whether inherited or acquired, are unhealthy because they cannot use their bodies as they desire? No. If someone is physically challenged, but is maximizing the use of his or her bodily functions, then he or she is both healthy *and* inspiring.

> All of our three bodies should be balanced and in optimal condition for us to be healthy.

When we talk about health, many people think of young people with their flexible muscles and vibrant, smooth skin. To achieve this image of health, many older people exercise excessively or undergo plastic surgery to eliminate wrinkles. But a true standard of health should not be measured against the attributes of youth. It is foolish to expect a 70-year-old to be as flexible and strong as a 20-year-old. Rather, health is a matter of maintaining a level of vitality that is appropriate for our age. No one can avoid aging, even if they're healthy when they're young. As you get older, the vitality and functioning of your body are bound to decline, and you are apt to start creaking here and there. Also, as you live your life, you could develop diseases great and small. Ultimately, we all die. We must be able to accept that dispassionately. What's important is a healthy mind. We lead our bodies with our minds. A healthy, flexible mind that can actively manage the health of the body, even as it accepts bodily realities dispassionately: this is the key to health.

The same principle applies to mental health. Should we say that a person is mentally healthy simply because he or she is free of diagnosed mental diseases? For true mental health, we must have a sufficient understanding of the functions and workings of our minds and must be able to make use of them. The mind has attributes that are much more sophisticated and amazing than those of the body. How deeply do you understand the functions of your mind, and how well do you use them? Are you the master of your mind, or a slave to its constant ruminations?

If a person fails to become the master of her mind and is led about by the whims of the mind, then she is not really a mentally healthy person. Using your mind as you desire means utilizing your thoughts and emotions well for your own purposes. Thus, we can say "mental health" is a state in which one can effectively apply the functions and energy of the mind.

We cannot say that a person is in a state of complete health just because he is physically and mentally healthy. If you avoid personal relationships, social activities, or engage in actions that have a negative impact on society, that can all be unhealthy. A healthy person must be socially healthy: able to contribute to the health of the community through positive personal relationships and social activities.

A healthy person must be able to use her body and mind as she intends for her own purposes. What, then, are desirable intentions and purposes? What should she use her body and mind for if we are to call her "healthy?" Such a definition of health includes two fundamental questions. The first question is, "Who am I?" The second is, "What is the purpose of my life?" These questions are directly related to spirituality and the growth of consciousness. And this concept expands and goes to another level, from that of health of body and mind to health on a spiritual level. Though a person is free of any physical or mental ailments and enjoys positive personal relationships and social activities, she is not genuinely healthy unless she obtains spiritual satisfaction.

> A healthy person must be able to use her body and mind as she intends for her own purposes.

Taking all of this into consideration, we can expand the conventional definition of health to mean "the state of knowing clearly who I am and what the purpose of my life is, and the ability to make the most of my body and mind for achieving that purpose." True well-being includes health of the body, the mind, and even the soul.

Health is not a matter of purely individual consideration. With a deeper understanding of life, health of the individual expands outward to society, to humanity, and to the earth. It means individual health is closely connected to the health of the external environment. Everyone is affected by their outward environment—whether it is their family, community, country, the human society, or even the planet.

It is inevitable that the health of the citizens in a country will be poor if there are poor economic conditions, or if political corruption is so bad that their human rights are not protected. People living in a city with severe air pollution cannot be expected to maintain good physical or mental health. No matter how hard we try to be healthy as individuals, we cannot avoid being affected by the health of the communities in which we live.

The health of the individual reflects the health of the whole. Similarly, we live among organic, interdependent relationships in which the health of the whole influences the health of the individual. For individuals and society to be healthy, we must recognize that we are not separate, but form one integrated organism. When we experience the essence of life through Ki, life energy, we come to understand the interdependence of the universe.

Principle of Good Health

Understanding the principles of Ki allows us to maintain health of body and mind. Try this—touch your forehead with your hand right now. Is your forehead cooler or warmer than your hand? Or is it much hotter? If your condition is normal, your forehead shouldn't be much hotter than your hand. Some people observe that their forehead has never felt cooler than their hand. This condition is due to constant stress-induced heating of the head. Try feeling your forehead when you wake up after a good night's sleep. Your forehead will definitely be cooler than your hand.

The principle of Suseung Hwagang describes the normal and

balanced state of Ki in the human body and is observed when the temperature of the head is cool and the abdomen is warm. Translated literally, Suseung Hwagang means "water rises, fire sinks," which I often refer to as Water Up, Fire Down. Our bodies contain both the warm energy of fire and the cool energy of water. If your energy is balanced, water energy will rise to your head, keeping it cool, and fire energy will settle in your abdomen, keeping it warm. In essence, you will have a cool head and fire in the belly. When this condition exists, your body will be able to maintain a condition of optimal health.

We can easily observe the phenomenon of Suseung Hwagang in nature as well. The radiant heat of the sun pours down onto the earth, illustrating the phenomenon of Hwagang, fire sinks. Cooked by the heat of the sun, water evaporates to become vapor that rises toward the sky, illustrating the phenomenon of Suseung, water rises. The earth's water resources are caused by the interchange of "falling fire" and "rising water." All plants, animals, and humans, are provided heat and water to maintain life. The circulation of fire and water is a fundamental principle of life on earth, and when this principle operates properly in the body, we are naturally healthy.

> Suseung Hwagang describes the normal and balanced state of Ki in the human body.

In the body, the energy of water is located in the kidneys, and the energy of fire is located in the heart. When fire energy (heat) is accumulated in the lower abdomen, it circulates throughout the entire body. The warm energy flows downward to the lower back, where it warms the kidneys, pushing water energy upward. Once it rises to the head, the cool water energy pushes the warm fire energy downward from the head, heart, and liver, and into the lower abdomen, further heating its energy. When your energy is flowing smoothly, this process circulates endlessly.

When the principle of Suseung Hwagang is activated, the head becomes cooler, allowing the brain to concentrate and fully use its capabilities for creation. When the lower abdomen becomes warmer, the functioning and activity of the abdominal organs are improved. Also sweet-tasting saliva collects in the mouth.

When your Suseung Hwagang circulation is disrupted, too much hot energy accumulates in the head, causing such symptoms as headaches, dry mouth, and an irregular heartbeat. A general feeling of malaise develops, often accompanied by weariness, anxiety and stiffness in the neck and shoulders. When the fire energy in the head and heart fails to sink, the belly grows colder, resulting in stiffness in the intestines, abdominal pain, and other digestive problems. As the energy flow continues to be blocked, other conditions such as constipation, cold hands and feet, lack of sexual energy, and high blood pressure may result.

Generally, poor Suseung Hwagang circulation can be caused by two factors. One is that the Dahnjon has not been trained and developed well enough to hold fire energy. Many people in our modern society use their heads too much and move their bodies too little, causing the fire energy to stay in their heads. Another reason is that the mind is consumed by stress and too focused on negative emotions. The result is blockage in the chest, which produces a reversal of the normal flow of energy: fire energy, which should sink, instead rises to the head.

Restoring proper Suseung Hwagang circulation will correct the symptoms that develop when the flow of Ki is reversed. It is as simple as correcting whatever prevents Suseung Hwagang. In other words, all you have to do is control stress and negative emotions as you strengthen your core, Dahnjon, which will provide enough power to open a path for energy flow and promote proper energy circulation. Also, if you release blockages in places where they commonly occur, such as the chest, shoulders, neck, and lower back, and soften stiff or-

> **Keep your head cool and your lower abdomen warm!**

gans so you can breathe deeply, then the heat in your head, heart, and liver will gradually sink, your lower abdomen will grow warmer, and you will return to a state of Suseung Hwagang.

So remember—keep your head cool and your lower abdomen warm! Suseung Hwagang is a fundamental principle of life and an index of health. If you invest an hour in yourself, or at least thirty minutes a day, and train diligently to ensure that energy can circulate well in your body, it will really help you develop and maintain good health.

Sexuality

What are your thoughts about sex? Do you think sex is beautiful in your head, but in your heart feel shame or guilt around sex? Do you enjoy sex, or avoid it? Usually, a person's attitudes and experiences around sex have significant impact on the quality of their life and their intimate relationships. Many people have distorted views or double standards regarding sex. In many cases, this reality acts as a great stumbling block, preventing them from living fully complete lives.

Sexual desire is animalistic in nature, but at the same time may also express that which is sacred. Many people are still very narrow-minded in their thoughts about sexuality. We should expand our understanding of this amazing energy and actively apply it because sexual desire is an important part of life. If we sublimate sexual desire and make it a spiritual strength rather than just a sensual pleasure, our attitudes about sexual energy can change in ground-breaking ways.

Sexual desire is the most intense longing we experience, because of the dual forces of Yin and Yang in the universe. It exists everywhere and helps create balance. For example, the earth is Yin, and heaven is Yang. Likewise, the night is Yin, and the day is Yang. Yin is the feminine force, while Yang is the masculine force.

The world is set into motion through the interaction of Yin and Yang energy. Many organisms are born into this world through an encounter of Yin and Yang energy. This applies to human beings. Woman has Yin energy and man has Yang energy; it is instinctual and natural that these two beings search for their other half. A new life is born when Yin meets Yang, Yang meets Yin, and the two become one.

From a biological standpoint, the longing to experience sexual pleasure is natural and engraved deeply in our brains. Over the course of millions of years of evolution, we have developed a surprisingly sophisticated system of neural pathways and hormonal controls. Through this system, members of the human species have found partners for whom they felt positive emotions and sexual attraction.

Neuroscientists say that, to a large degree, even love between people is an emotion felt as a result of brain activity. Hunger is generated according to the levels of glucose, which is the brain's one and only energy source. In the same way, sexual desire is also generated according to the concentration of sex hormones, and scientists say that even the emotion we call "love" occurs as a result of the action of neurotransmitters secreted in the brain.

In the beginning stages of love, just looking at the other person makes us feel good because of the actions of the neurotransmitter dopamine. Then, at the stage when the hormone oxytocin is secreted, the sexual need to embrace the person we love occurs. Once that time passes, as endorphins are secreted, we bask in the joy and happiness of love, and arrive at love's stable period. Similar to the drug morphine, endorphins are hormones that eliminate pain and cause a sense of happiness. According to the results of one scientific study, activity in the insula, anterior cingulate cortex, caudate nucleus, and putamen increase in the brain in love. Noteworthy is that these are the same parts of the brain that are excited when a person is stimulated by illegal drugs. Love, like a kind of drug, causes a person to become addicted because it puts our brains into ecstasy. To put it another way, it is our brains that like sex.

> We can have mature experiences on sex when we accept it as a natural phenomenon.

Society often promotes old-fashioned beliefs about sex that make us feel guilty. Throughout history, sexual shame and guilt have been deeply ingrained in human consciousness. Excessively moralistic norms restrict individual consciousness, ultimately standing in the way of personal happiness. We are often tormented by the disconnect between sexual morality and sexual needs, and we get caught up in humiliation. The consciousness of those who feel shame and guilt about sex cannot grow properly.

Human nature is always natural. There is no need to attach descriptions like "vulgar" or "noble." All life begins in sex. We would not be here unless sexual intercourse had taken place. We can have mature experiences concerning sex only when our value systems and attitudes accept it as a natural phenomenon.

Sexual desire is also a very intense need, and thus we should make careful judgments in its expression. We can hurt others through sexual behavior that involves attempts to dominate the other person, or if our desire rages out of control. Moreover, once sex becomes an addiction, it robs us of rich personal relationships.

Depending on what choices we make and what values we hold, sex can generate intimacy or it can become an indulgence. Mature sex is healing, and it can become a means of genuine communication between two people's bodies and minds. The human is a multidimensional being with three bodies: a physical body, an energy body, and a spiritual body. Consequently, mature sexuality accompanies experience on the level of all three of these bodies. In other words, sexual relations involve energetic and spiritual communion through mutual respect and open-mindedness; they're not something that ends at the level of simply satisfying physical needs.

Although an effect of hormones, sexual desire is simultaneously a longing of the soul for oneness. Two different people experience a moment in which their sense of separation completely vanishes by their becoming one within a powerful flow of life. They experience feelings of unity and ecstasy, forgetting everything for a short moment, through sex, but it fails to resolve their fundamental loneliness as human beings. Addiction to sex to avoid the emptiness and loneliness of life, like drinking alcohol to forget immediate worries, is definitely undesirable. The fundamental loneliness that humans feel is not resolved through the experience of romantic love. In some ways, this love is like licking honey off the edge of a sharp blade. You'll be okay if you lick it very gently, but get too greedy and the blade cuts your tongue. Such love comes with all sorts of emotional traps, including envy, jealousy, hatred, and attachment.

Managing well and making good use of sexual energy is a good Tao practice. Sexual energy can be converted to passionate, creative energy for other activities. Every time we feel sexual desire, we can't very well release it through sexual relations the way we drink when we're thirsty or eat when we're hungry? The waves of sexual energy subside if the energy of the body circulates well through full concentration on creative, fulfilling work or through exercise that moves the body. When it isn't converted into energy for other activities, though, sexual energy travels around the whole body, creating all kinds of sexual fantasies and desires.

> Sexual energy can be converted to passionate, creative energy for other activities.

At such times, it's good to train the Dahnjon through energy training, like yoga and kigong, or to charge the energy of the Dahnjon through deep energy breathing. It's easy to think that it would be hard to control sexual desire when the Dahnjon and the lower chakras are charged with energy. But actually, the less energy people have in their Dahnjon, the more they tend to indulge in or become addicted to sex because their power to control their sexual needs is weakened.

When sexual energy is converted into active energy and a strong core forms in the Dahnjon through training, it prevents sexual energy from wandering to every part of the body or rising to the head to elicit sexual thoughts, and this makes it easier to control sexual needs. Sexual energy converted into active energy brings passion for life and vitality to living. It becomes a kind of fertilizer for positive social action as well as for creative activities like the arts, writing, and music.

Also, sexual energy is not necessarily something that can be resolved solely through a physical relationship with a partner, using the energy of the lower Dahnjon. The Ki energy of the middle Dahnjon can also be used for this purpose, as can the Shin energy of the upper Dahnjon.

When you use the energy of the middle Dahnjon, a deep energy exchange, every bit as powerful as sexual relations, occurs just by taking the other person's hand or giving them a warm embrace. When you use the energy of the upper Dahnjon, communion occurs even with nothing more than deep gazing into each other's eyes. You can also give and receive energy consciously through meditation, even if the other person isn't in front of you.

Ultimately, our brains can obtain deep, genuine, lasting satisfaction through an exchange of life energy with the cosmos, which is not the level of exchanging energy with a person through sex. If human energy is Yin, then cosmic energy is Yang. Once we develop an energy sense, we can experience the numinous energy of the cosmos entering through the crown of our head to charge the energy of our upper, middle, and lower Dahnjon. Then the hole in us created by a fundamental emptiness and loneliness is finally filled and, through the powerful support of cosmic energy, the energy of joy, love, and vitality can overflow in our hearts. This is a new sense transcending the level of the five senses, which takes place in the world of energy.

Human beings intuit that there is a world beyond the reach of the five senses. When we recover our full range of senses, we will no longer be dominated by the desire for sex, but will instead become its master, able to commune with the true nature of the great cosmos, the Tao.

Money

What are your ideas about money? Is money important to you? Why or why not? Do you think you have enough money or too little? What is the purpose of money with regard to your spiritual growth?

If you gave a hundred-dollar bill to a person living somewhere distant from modern civilization, he or she would think of it as little more than a piece of paper. But, if you scattered hundred-dollar bills on the street in any major city, pandemonium would result when everyone rushed to grab as many bills as he or she could. On the surface, a hundred-dollar bill is no more than a piece of paper, but that scrap of paper has enormous power behind it in the minds of most people in the material world. To many, money means power, and power means the freedom to live life however one chooses.

> What is the purpose of money with regard to your spiritual growth?

Money was originally a means of assessing value, a medium of exchange, a means of payment, and a means of storing value. Lately, however, money has become not a means, but an end in itself. We define our worth and evaluate our abilities by how much money we make. We believe other people evaluate our worth based on our bank account. There seem to be more people suffering because of money in modern society, even though it is much better off materially than societies of long ago.

Many people have a double standard when it comes to money.

In reality, everyone needs it and wants as much as they can get, yet they look upon those who have more money than they do as somehow evil or greedy. The idea of money is especially conflicted among spiritual growth circles because many believe you should not have to pay for spirituality, but even the most revered spiritual teachers need money to support their most basic needs.

For many, our beliefs about money and the necessity to have it for our basic survival are contradictory views. We often have negative associations with money and feel insecure in our ability to realize our monetary dreams. Such discomfort weakens our motivation to earn money and hinders proactive, creative action.

Another contradictory attitude toward people is fear. The fears that our abilities are evaluated through money, and that our financial risks may result in our being assessed as "economic failures," also weaken our motivation to earn money and inhibit us from taking positive action.

We are often so conflicted in our beliefs about money that we seldom examine our beliefs closely to determine whether they are supporting or hindering our life's purpose. In order to master your life around money, it is important to look at your internal limitations and develop core principles that will help you deal with money in a more proactive manner.

First, you must remain true to your values and priorities. Never violate your personal values or principles simply in order to get money. This may involve adopting such traits as always acting with honesty, integrity, and compassion in how you make your money; not doing harm to others; and being transparent in your goals and objectives.

To avoid getting caught up in inner conflict, it may be helpful to establish clear priorities in terms of your values and to remain true to those principles. For example, perhaps you have established your values to be truth, goodness, and beauty—in that order. In that case, all your actions and decisions around money should never abandon truth for the sake of goodness, or goodness for the sake of beauty. If you've established such principles but fail to remain true to them, you will eventually feel shame or a sense of failure. Someday, you will recognize that you sacrificed your principles for the sake of money.

Although individual circumstances differ from person to person, we all experience money issues sometime during our lives. These experiences can weaken our motivation around money and undermine our potential for economic success. In the long term, they can also erode our sense of self-esteem. If you honestly establish your own priorities, then you will be able to deal with money difficulties with

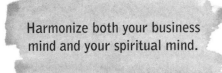

Harmonize both your business mind and your spiritual mind.

more ease and greater peace of mind, knowing that in the end, if you remain true to your principles, everything will work out fine.

Second, have a clear goal in relation to money, one that is able to satisfy your conscience and convince your brain of its usefulness. Would you have a clear answer if someone were to ask you what your goal was for earning money? It's difficult to get what you want without a clear goal, no matter what it is you're doing.

For lasting satisfaction, you must harmonize both your business mind and your spiritual mind in regard to the issue of money. Many people live their lives working diligently with only a business mind. To determine whether this is true for you, ask yourself, "Do you seek money just for your own sake, or do you have a vision for sharing it with others? How will you contribute to a better society if you have more money? Can you make a meaningful contribution in the lives of others even if you have limited monetary resources?" If you genuinely want to work not only merely to profit yourself and your family, but also to help the community to which you belong and even more people besides, then we can say that you have a spiritual mind. Although you may pursue material interests with a business mind, when it is supported by a spiritual mind that seeks goodness for all, those material interests end up creating spiritual value.

The mind that views both the material and the spiritual as an organic whole and that can use matter to manifest a spiritually sound reality is a genuine spiritual mind.

How you use money is far more important than how much you have. There are many great business people in this world who earn money with honesty, sincerity, and a sense of responsibility and who contribute the money they've earned to society by using it for the health and welfare of many people.

The concept of "ownership" is actually false because we come to the earth with empty hands and leave it with empty hands. Everything I own I got when I came to this planet; I've *borrowed* it all temporarily from the earth for my use. We even have to give back our physical bodies to the earth once we've used them. Thus, our task is to make the best possible use of them while we are here.

Money itself is neither good nor bad. What's important is the consciousness of the person using the money. The money of someone with a good consciousness will be used to benefit others and society, while the money of someone with a greedy consciousness will continuously trample the happiness of others. So the more money good people have, the better, and the more money evil people have, the worse. The more money that gathers to good people and good organizations, the more powerful their energy becomes for changing the world.

That's why I tell young people to go after money and power with everything they've got. They can do a lot of good with these things as long as the proper spirit lives within them and is the motivating factor behind their pursuit of these things. Those who have a clear philosophy and the spirit of philanthropy, and the will and self-control

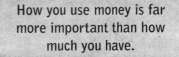

How you use money is far more important than how much you have.

to remain true to that spirit to the end, can give a lot of hope to the world and its people. Those who have a spiritual mind but completely lack a business mind may be able to maintain a simple life, but they will find it difficult to actively pioneer a creative life.

You can choose how to deal with money—ignore it, saying it is unimportant; earn a lot of money but only for personal profit; or earn a lot and use it for the benefit of all those around you. Which of these do you want to do?

Fame

We seek fame consciously or unconsciously in our lives. Fame is often developed and maintained by receiving attention and recognition from those around us and in the world. Much of our daily activity involves a series of performances that are designed to generate acceptance from others. This need for acceptance and social recognition is innate, but it is further reinforced throughout life.

During childhood, we behave in ways that will generate love and recognition from our parents. At school, we study hard to get praise from our teachers, and perform socially to gain acceptance from our peers. As we grow older, we put a great deal of effort into getting recognition as an excellent employee and, after we get married, as a good spouse, and as a good parent in the eyes of our children. Additionally, the external appearance we work so hard to cultivate as we stare into the mirror every day can be viewed as a part of our efforts to get love and recognition, as well as self-satisfaction.

Our efforts toward winning the love and acknowledgement of those around us may continuously accumulate over time to make us who we are.

The need for recognition, along with the need for security and control, create the human emotions of happiness and unhappiness. We are happier and thrilled when we get interest and recognition from those around us. For example, the little forms of praise you get from those around you for your new hairstyle or for the food you cook bring a smile to your face. There's no need to elaborate on how thrilled you are by the compliments you receive when the project you've been pursuing greatly succeeds.

As a form of energy, the interest and recognition people send us fills us with overflowing confidence and powerful energy. The energy that goodwill and being popular give us is incredibly fascinating. When we consider that the smiles on our faces and our growing confidence directly relate to the number of likes our friends give the posts and photos we upload to social media, we realize that such posts may be our attempts to receive that energy.

When the energy people send you gradually expands, making you more popular, that fame attracts money and power. Online content that receives a great many views is followed by more advertising revenue, and the people who created that content become famous. We are fascinated with the wealth and power that attaches to well-known entertainers, amazing athletes, successful businesspeople, and professional politicians. We cheer and applaud them, and the louder our acclamations grow, the higher their incomes rise.

The world can be divided into two categories: people who get applause and people who give it. We first experience that distinction when we are young and in school. A few children are applauded because they are smart, or are talented athletes or artists; the majority of children give them applause. Do you remember which category you belonged to? Such classification does not end with our school years, though. As we live our lives in a society of infinite competition, we're bound to be divided into winners and losers, into those giving applause and those receiving it.

> Another reason we pursue fame is to confirm our own existential value.

When we watch famous stars on television, we applaud them and envy their wonderful appearances and fabulous lifestyles. Not everyone can be like those stars, like successful businesspeople or politicians. Why? Because such wealth and fame are limited values obtainable through fierce competition, arduous work and occasionally good fortune. To obtain such limited values, we have to leap into the battle to reach the peak of a mountain where very few easy chairs are placed. Those who don't want that competition, or who have been washed out of it, live their lives applauding others. Do most people have to go on with lives lived enviously applauding others? Aren't there values other than social success and fame that we should pursue?

Another reason we pursue fame is to confirm our own existential value. As social beings, we feel our existential value increasing when we get interest and recognition from others. Imagine it. How would you feel if no one you knew gave you interest, love, or recognition? Your pride and existential value would gradually decrease, and you would become discouraged and depressed. In contrast with this, the wealth and power that come with fame greatly increase the existential value of people, and they feel themselves to be Very Important Persons.

Among the famous stars who once lived surrounded by wealth and fame are some who fall into depression and drug addiction. Some even choose the extreme of suicide when their popularity declines. This easily happens to those who consider fame the standard measure of their own existential value. They feel themselves to be very important persons when they are famous, but end up feeling as if their existential value vanishes when their popularity drops. This is because they focus solely on how other people evaluate them. Because they pay attention only to how others react to them, their vision inevitably turns to the outside, and the continuous repetition of this ends up causing them to be cut off from their own inner selves. Being cut off from yourself causes great unhappiness.

No matter how much people recognize you, or how popular you are with them, you will be unhappy unless you acknowledge yourself. True recognition does not only come from those around you or the world. It comes when you recognize and love yourself.

Ask yourself this: Have I acknowledged and loved myself? Have I tormented myself by comparing my abilities, appearance, and environment with those of others and asking myself, "Am I nothing more than this?" Have I pursued what I truly wanted to do and truly wanted to become? Or, conscious of what others think, have I sought to become what they wanted?

Many people neglect acknowledging and loving themselves, even as they put a great deal of effort into getting recognition and love from others. If you live your life always conscious only of what others think, you'll end up rushing about as if pursued, and at some point the thought will come to you that you have no life. You'll live 20, 30, even 60 years dragging about your body, unable to answer the questions, "Why do I always feel so empty?" and "What is my true self?" Those who think, "Living is that way for everyone, you know. That's life,

> True recognition comes when you recognize and love yourself.

isn't it?" are incapable of change. There is hope, though, for those who think, "I don't know what it is, but doesn't something exist that's greater than what I feel and experience now? Is the life I've been living thus far the best it can be?"

To acknowledge and love ourselves, we have to discover what our true existential value is. Fame and social success are not standards of measure for determining the success of our lives. They are limited values obtainable only by a minority, so they are inadequate as absolute values everyone should pursue. That something that is accessible to anyone with effort, and without any need to compete with others, should be the essential condition for the true existential value for which we must aim. We absolutely cannot find it in the finite, material world. We can find it inside ourselves, in the unseen world of the spirit. It is our true self, our soul. Continuing to grow the energy of the soul in our hearts, and sharing the fragrance of that soul with those around us, is the true absolute value and purpose that brings us fundamental satisfaction and joy.

No matter how hard you try, you can never fill your empty heart solely with energy received through external recognition or success, for these are but temporary comforts. They are not eternal. You can discover within yourself a wellspring of eternal energy. That energy will start to spring forth when you acknowledge and love yourself. The joy you feel from acknowledging yourself is so great that it cannot be compared with the joy you feel from getting recognition from others. This is a matter of being recognized by your conscience and the heaven within you.

You don't acknowledge and love yourself just by thinking about it. You must encounter the life energy within you. Slowly place your hands on your chest, one over the other. Now say this to yourself: "Yes, I have myself. I have myself, who always watches over me, the one who is always on my side no matter what may come. It's my soul and my true self. It is my eternally unchanging life." If you speak to yourself with sincerity, you'll be able to feel the energy of the soul inside you, the energy of life, reviving.

Those who know the true self within them are never afraid or lonely, no matter what may come. Their hearts are filled to overflowing with energy from the feeling of oneness with themselves, as if they possess the whole world. Whenever you feel lonely, whenever you want recognition from someone, continue to meet the true self within your heart repeating, "Yes, I have myself." And never forget to set aside a part of your time and energy to the existential values you put first and consider most important. The tree of life, your soul, will grow strong, bloom with beautiful flowers, and bear good fruit to the extent it gets your interest, love, and recognition.

In Chapter 10, we'll deal separately with the last of our five subjects, death.

CHAPTER SEVEN

Five Character Traits for the Growth of the Soul

GIVEN THAT THE SOUL IS INVISIBLE, what should you do to grow it, and how can you witness and measure its growth? The only thing that reveals the condition of your soul is your personal character. Character is expressed through interpersonal relationships. Essentially, character is the soul manifested through relationships. Although your soul cannot tangibly be perceived, your character clearly shows the extent to which your soul has grown. We depend on our relationships, our communities, and our roles and responsibilities to provide us with opportunities to develop and grow our souls.

In our relationships with other people, we make choices, take action according to those choices, and evaluate the results of those actions. This process provides opportunities for self-reflection and cultivates the wisdom to make better choices in the future. Our thinking changes, our behavior changes, and our habits change in the course of choosing, acting, reflecting, and then choosing again.

Although it can hurt to experience painful relationships with others, it is through these struggles that we grow more rapidly. By reflecting on those relationships, we can observe our habits and motivations, both positive and negative. We can set clear goals about the kind of person we want to be and slowly work to change our habits, and our relationships as a result. In this process, we develop a virtuous character that acts harmoniously with others.

Your spiritual growth is demonstrated by the character traits you exhibit in your relationships. When you show compassion, tolerance, openness and gratitude toward others, when you act with honesty, sincerity, and responsibility, you are demonstrating a higher level of consciousness and actively engaging in your spiritual growth.

As your level of consciousness increases, you become increasingly more aware of your thoughts, behaviors, and actions, and the impact they have on others. You are able to see your character traits with more objectivity and more clearly identify those that you want to change. This inner awakening is essential for transforming your outer world. It governs the development of your character and the social relationships that impact your spiritual growth.

If you go to a bookstore, you'll find many books on how to deal with life. Many authors introduce their methods as secrets to success. Most of those books deal with techniques necessary for success, and they introduce various detailed, concrete tools. Of course, many of those tools are useful and commendable. But even the most sophisticated techniques or well-crafted tools are not very effective if they don't include a change of character produced through growth of consciousness.

> Your spiritual growth is demonstrated by the character traits you exhibited in your relationships.

If you seek to change your external packaging without changing the inside, eventually, who you are on the inside is bound to be revealed, even if you have been successful in the short run. And since you are aware of the inconsistency between your inner reality and outer appearance, you won't be bold and confident in front of others. You'll be worried about being found out, and you will put on a show in order to conceal who you are on the inside. Enduring such discomfort is not easy, and ultimately you will give up and show yourself for who you used to be.

Most failures in relationships and leadership are due to this dissonance. Consequently, if you genuinely want to live a successful life, inner awakening must precede any external improvement. And, through such an awakening, you must achieve growth of consciousness and change of character.

How to Develop Good Character

People commonly think that developing good character means adding something new that wasn't there before. For example, a person might resolve to change and add the element of "friendliness" to her character. She may say to herself, "I've never been a friendly person. I've hardly ever smiled, and I get angry a lot. From now on, though, I'll be a friendly person." In order to fulfill her resolution, she smiles intentionally and tries to use a friendly manner of speaking. She works hard at it, but feels awkward saying and doing things differently while building a new habit that doesn't match her previous behavior.

It would be easier for her to express friendliness if she knew that building good character isn't about adding something new that you've never had before. It's about developing an existing expression within you that has always been there. You have always had positive character traits like "friendliness" within you. Building character means finding those traits inside and letting them show.

How can you be sure you have a character trait you've never expressed in your life? Because good character is an expression of the soul, and everyone has a soul. The seed of a good character is already within your soul, and all you have to do is find and grow it.

The Korean word for character is *Maeumssi*. Maeumssi means the "seed (Ssi) of the mind or heart (Maeum)." You often hear Korean people say, "Your Maeumssi should be good. You need to grow your Maeumssi." This means developing your character, the seed of your soul.

How does a person develop good character? First, a good environment lays the foundation. Just as good-quality soil, suitable sunlight, and water enable a seed to sprout, so too does our character sprout and grow in a good environment. The environment that is most important in developing good human character is the family. In the same way that plants are grown with love and devotion, the seed of a beautiful character grows amid the love and interest of parents who care for the hearts and minds of their children.

According to the experiment of Dr. Masaru Emoto, water is influenced by the human mind and its immediate environment. In his experiment, people praised one cup of water for its beauty, played beautiful music for it, and supplied it with plenty of good air. People told a different cup of water how much it was hated and despised, played dark, depressing music for it, and left it in a poor environment. Water that was in the positive environment had beautiful, hexagonal crystals like snowflakes, while water that was in the negative environment had sharp, jagged crystals.

If the energy of the mind has such an influence on mere water, think about the impact that people's thoughts and words have on young children. "Is that all you can do? I wonder who you take after!" This kind of talk drives like an arrow deep into the consciousness of the child. Such information occupies a place in the brain, becoming a fixed

> The seed of a good character is already within your soul.

idea. Most of your conceptions of self are formed in childhood— what you think about yourself, what you think about those around you, what you think about the world, what you expect others to think of you, and so on. Beliefs ingrained into the mind during childhood can have conscious and subconscious effects throughout our entire lives.

Thus, parents have the greatest influence on the formation of the fixed mental concepts that follow us into adulthood. We automatically begin to take the way they see the world as their own before we are even aware that we are beings separate from others. In addition, other family members, school teachers, friends, and media such as TV, movies, and video games all play an important role in laying this foundation.

The influence of environment on our character is shown by the famous story of the fourth-century BCE scholar, Mencius. Mencius inherited and further developed the teachings of Confucius about a century after the famous thinker died.

Mencius's father died when he was young, so he was raised and educated by his mother. The two of them first lived near a public cemetery, where Mencius often saw people holding funerals. Whenever he played with his friends, the boy pretended to wail or dig a grave and perform a funeral.

Witnessing this, Mencius's mother thought the environment of the cemetery was not good for her child's education, so they moved near a market. Soon, during play, Mencius was pretending to be a merchant buying and selling goods. Mencius's mother wanted her son to become an educated scholar, so she again moved, this time to a place near a village school.

Within a short time, when Mencius played, he acted as if he were reading, bowing, and performing rituals for the ancestors. At the time, schools taught the Confucian ritual of holding memorial services for the ancestors. On seeing this, Mencius's mother settled down there, concluding it was the best place for her son's education.

The story of Mencius shows just how important the surrounding environment is for a child's life and education and how easily children are influenced by it. It demonstrates how the pure brains of children are especially designed to model the environment to which they are exposed and incorporate the information to which they have access into their worldviews. Information that leaves a powerful impression on a child may even influence his or her entire life. Everyone has childhood experiences that helped mold the formation of his or her present personality or character.

Our childhood environments, like family and school, were given to us; we had no say in the matter. Whether their influence on us was good or bad, we cannot deny that those environments were the foundation upon which our present character and ideas were built. Rather than blaming our childhood environments, it's useful to look back on what influence they had in the formation of who we are now. The environments given to each of us are grist for the mill in our studies for the growth of our souls. Just as lotus flowers bloom out of murky, muddy water, so can the struggles and suffering we feel in difficult environments be the sustenance that causes our souls to grow.

> **Develop your character through ceaseless choosing.**

Environment continues to be important throughout life. People's characters are frequently influenced by their friends, the careers they choose, and the organizations or groups to which they belong. If you know the importance of your environment, you can be more cautious when you choose it.

Although the environment has great influence on the development of a person's character, that character is not unchanging. We can definitely create good character if we make up our minds to work at it. Besides creating a good enviroment, another method for developing good character is making consistently good choices. Although environment is important, it is even more important to develop your character through ceaseless choosing instead of simply blaming your surroundings, regardless of what they may be. I often mention Benjamin Franklin as a vivid illustration of this principle.

Benjamin Franklin completed only two years of elementary school. He was the fifteenth of seventeen children and his family was not affluent. At the age of 12, his domestic circumstances spurred him to take employment at his brother's printing press. After just a year or two, Ben became so competent that he had nothing more to learn about working there. He devoted himself to his own self-development and learned to speak three languages, gaining a command of French and Spanish. At the age of 18, he became the publisher of a newspaper.

Ben continued to study and gain expertise in many fields. As a scientist, he discovered the principles of electrical discharge and invented such things as the lightning rod and the Franklin stove (still produced today); he left a great legacy as one of the earliest American politicians, including the pivotal role he played by forging an alliance with France in the American movement for independence.

His work brought him into contact with people from all walks of life, including politicians, presidents, entrepreneurs, and educators, and he realized that there was something more important than being rich, famous, and powerful. In his twenties, he decided that the goal of his life would be to cultivate his character. To that end, he created and followed a list of 13 virtues that included Temperance, Humility, and Sincerity.

Because he lived by those principles, he earned trust from those around him and naturally achieved accomplishments in diverse fields as a politician, diplomat, writer, entrepreneur, journalist, philosopher, and educator. As a leader, he became a role model for self-development. Benjamin Franklin was the quintessential example of his all-too-famous motto: "Never leave that till tomorrow which you can do today."

Despite his many accomplishments, for his tombstone he chose only the words "Benjamin Franklin, Printer." With that simple description, he acknowledged that he was just another laborer and showed himself to be a humble person of true character; he exemplified how a human being should live.

Another reason for his greatness is that, despite his poor surroundings, he committed himself tirelessly to self-development. He showed that it isn't necessary to be taught how to do things, but that you can figure things out for yourself, and that it is possible to dedicate yourself to self-development by choosing it and making the effort regardless of your occupation or academic record.

> Character is not something that we can buy with money, power, or fame.

Deeply moved by Benjamin Franklin's life and philosophy, I created the Benjamin School of Character Education in Korea several years ago. Instead of providing education centered on conveying knowledge, the core objective of the school is to enable students to develop their own creative lives by refining their character and discovering their own existential value.

Character is not something that we can buy with money, power, or fame. Nor can it be created with knowledge. Rather, it comes as we gain confidence in ourselves. We gain deep trust in ourselves when we make good choices. We discover our own inherent worth, and find a sense of satisfaction in who we have become. No one can take that feeling from us. If we have not developed good character, it cannot be camouflaged. A person may be outwardly kind and honest when people are looking, but true character is revealed when you add up all 24 hours in the day.

Your soul appears suddenly in the process of developing good character. Various good character traits come from your soul as it was originally, from out of your true nature. In the same way, as you develop those traits, your true nature is naturally illuminated.

Our souls are nurtured by the trust and joy we gain while developing our character. When we overcome the body's selfish desires, we cultivate the good habits that lead to good character. The light of your character illuminates your soul, sheds light on the souls of others, and allows you to perceive the beauty that is all around you. Only those who have deeply moved their own souls can see genuine beauty in others and in the world.

What kind of character traits, then, are needed to grow our souls? There are many good character traits, but five are essential as a foundation for the growth of the soul: honesty, sincerity, responsibility, courtesy, and faithfulness. Without these five basic traits, you cannot walk the path toward the completion of your soul. Even if you want to grow your soul, you will inevitably come up against significant limitations—or give up—unless you develop these five traits in the process.

A good basic character should be developed even before discussing enlightenment or the growth of your soul. That's why Zen initiates developed their basic character traits through nine years of study—three years of cleaning, three years of firewood collecting and cutting, and three years of cooking. Teachings on the Tao were transmitted only to those who had successfully cultivated such character in themselves.

Honesty

The first character trait essential to the growth of the soul is *honesty*. Honesty is synonymous with truthfulness, integrity, and frankness. It represents freedom from deceit or fraud. Honesty means that what you hold true on the inside is reflected in what you express on the outside. Honesty is usually associated with the expression "transparency" or "openness." It's like a transparent lake that has no impurities covering its surface; the water is so clear we can see all the way to the bottom. When something covers the surface, or the water is murky, we have no way of knowing what might be hidden below.

There are two types of dishonesty. First, there is conscious dishonesty. In other words, a person lies, knowing he is telling a lie. We fabricate things and disguise the truth in order to achieve our desires. Such lies may cause only small conflicts and discomfort in relationships with those around us, but they cause immense suffering when they build over time. Many of the events we see reported in the newspapers are negative outcomes of desire, such as an employee selling company secrets to a rival, a professor plagiarizing another person's work to gain prestige, or politicians using their power for personal gain. Compared with the outcomes of the desires of individuals, the effects of organizational desires may be unimaginably huge. Unfortunately, many organizations are built on dishonesty and lies designed to gain monetary profit.

> Our souls are nurtured by the trust and joy we gain while developing our character.

The second kind of dishonesty is more unconscious. Often we refer to this kind as "a little white lie." We've all told one or two (or more) in our lives. It's the lie that we justify in our minds because "it's not that big a deal" or because we don't want to hurt someone, or lose something we have. These kinds of benign lies are also dangerous, because they establish a behavior pattern over time that becomes ingrained in our character. We become more prone to telling bigger, more conscious lies, and still justify them in our minds. It is especially important, therefore, to become more aware of honesty as a character trait and work toward reflecting it in every aspect of our lives.

Lies told in a split second, without thinking, in order to avoid a crisis, come out unconsciously. They may be an unconscious form of self-defense. Below the surface, however, they are caused by our own dim perception of ourselves. This means that our consciousness is not bright enough to allow us to watch our own speech in the moment we speak the lies. We might expect this from young children whose identities or social consciousness is not sufficiently formed but, even as adults, dishonesty becomes habitual because our consciousness is not bright enough to illuminate what we are doing so that we can correct ourselves.

All forms of dishonesty, large and small, cast a veil over our true nature. This is why we must be honest in our practice and in working for the growth of our souls. To become honest, we must let go of our egoic desires, which are the sources of dishonesty. When we let go of our desires, and when we have nothing to hide, our need to deceive naturally vanishes. As we become more detached from our desires, we can cultivate the virtue of honesty in every aspect of our lives, and we can be more transparent with ourselves and others. This openness and transparency leads to better social relationships, which impact the growth of our soul.

Honesty is proportional to clarity of soul and brightness of consciousness. Being honest allows your soul to be clear and your consciousness to be bright. Genuine honesty, therefore, is not for winning recognition from others, but for getting recognition from ourselves and for recognizing our conscience within. Honesty makes us honorable in our own eyes.

Because we are human beings, we cannot expect ourselves to be perfect and faultless. We may occasionally make mistakes. But if we wish to achieve completion, we must be as honest as we can be. Cleaning and polishing our minds so that we have no shame in the light of our own conscience is the personification of Tao. Honesty is the foundational virtue for those who want to achieve the Tao.

Sincerity

Another character trait necessary for the growth of our souls is *sincerity*. Sincerity refers to a true, devoted attitude, to doing your best in the position and roles given to you.

Sincerity requires concentration that isn't scattered by any distraction, a consistent mind focused on one thing. It requires diligence even in the face of challenges. People who have it demonstrate wholehearted commitment to their beliefs. Working with sincerity brings rewards that are more valuable and precious than anything else in this world.

> Sincerity refers to a true, devoted attitude, to doing your best.

A famous story about a warrior illustrates the value of this virtue. When he was a young man, that warrior devoted himself to training diligently to master swordsmanship. But all he did was strike a wooden sword down onto a large stone about the height of a person's navel. From dawn until the deep darkness of night, he repeated just one movement without resting: the down strike. The warrior's heart became as strong and tenacious as the pile of broken swords was high and as his calluses were thick. One day, several  months later, in the instant he struck down forcefully with his wooden sword, the rock split in two. That warrior's constancy was so focused that it caused the rock to split in two. That power grew into physical and mental strength, a foundation that would later make him the greatest of warriors. A mind so consistent and focused that it can split solid rock is the result of *sincerity*.

We lose sincerity when we fail to focus on the present. But why do we fail to focus on the present? It is because we cannot find meaning in the roles and work we are performing. Our inability to find meaning leaves us dissatisfied with what we are doing or causes us to search for other work. Instead of focusing on the present, we waste our time lost in delusion and anguish, thinking, "I was successful in the past," or, "I will become such and such in the future."

There is no existence other than now, this moment. No matter how beautiful the past may have been, it has already passed. No matter how wonderful a future we suppose lies before us, it has not yet come. Apart from now, all is illusion. If you have a dream and want to acquire a better role and higher position, then you must escape from the delusion and anguish of your mind to concentrate on the present. If you want something better and higher, then you must create a footstool you can step on to reach it. You could end up tumbling to the floor if you try to grasp something higher without such a footstool. That base is created by concentrating on the present.

People with sincerity find meaning in what they're doing now, and dedicate themselves to actualize that meaning in each moment. Finding meaning in the spiritual rather than the material world strengthens the energy of the soul. When we do something that has spiritual meaning, even hard things don't seem difficult; they are recognized as a process through which the soul grows.

Another reason we fail to have sincerity is our desire for good luck. We hope not only for results commensurate with our efforts, but for outcomes greater than we deserve. It's reasonable for us to expect results equal to the amount of energy we have spent. Hoping for something beyond that—for a lucky winning lottery ticket, for example—distracts us from our present responsibilities and diminishes the mindset of sincerity.

Sincerity is a habit. It's not something you pretend to have in order to win the approval of others. It is something that comes out of your heart. Sincerity is not a trait you can wish for and have miraculously appear in just a few days. It is a disciplined way of living that becomes ingrained in your body through daily practice over a long period of time.

> Find meaning in what you are doing now, and dedicate yourselves to actualize that meaning.

People who have natural sincerity usually grew up with parents who demonstrated sincerity and diligence. Because they saw their parents rise early, work hard, and dedicate their minds to others or to their calling, they learned from an early age how to act.

When you're anxious about something or think your body condition is not good, you will be able to diagnose yourself in no time if you think, "Am I showing myself sincerity right now?" or, "What sort of sincerity have I shown those around me?" Those who have never experienced showing sincerity or devotion tend to feel anxious and impoverished love in their hearts.

Conversely, if you show sincerity to yourself, you can feel love, peace sprouts within, and vital energy overflows in your body. Personal relationships also inevitably improve for those who show sincerity to others. When you show sincerity first, trust develops, and anyone's heart is bound to open. Sincerity—this is the formula by which love for yourself and others develops.

Responsibility

The third character trait you need for the growth of your soul is *responsibility*. Responsibility refers to the notion of being accountable for one's actions or decisions. It reflects a reliability or dependability that you extend to others. It is the commitment to your duties and obligations; it is being answerable to yourself and others.

What responsibilities do you have? How do you work to fulfill them? Do you enjoy being responsible and accountable to others—your family, your co-workers, your friends—or do you find them burdensome and want to push them away?

When a person accepts responsibility, it means that he or she is accountable to society. Social roles signify social influence. By existing in this world, each person has an effect on others. The amount of social influence a person has depends on his or her level of responsibility. For example, the head of a family has a great impact on his or her family members, just as the mayor of a city influences all its citizens. A country's president affects all the citizens of that nation and, occasionally, those of other nations. In this way, the size and weight of a person's responsibility is equal to the amount of influence and power that person can exert.

Occasionally, having too many responsibilities can weigh so heavily on us that they become burdensome. If your responsibilities increase, you will have to use more energy than you have been using, and you will have to use your mind more effectively. Your consciousness must grow to become as bright and expansive as your responsibilities are large and weighty, because you will make your choices and decisions in accordance with your level of consciousness, and your decisions affect many people and influence important events. You need to acknowledge your interdependence with the world and make conscious choices about your actions.

> Responsibilities provide a platform for your purpose and an outlet to your energy.

You cannot realize your purpose in life, no matter how hard you try, without taking on a role and bearing responsibility for it. Responsibilities provide a platform for your purpose and an outlet to which you can commit your energy. As your consciousness grows sufficiently to suit your responsibilities, you can realize your true purpose, assist the people around you, and change society for the better. Therefore, instead of resisting a heavy burden, it is wise to accept it as a good opportunity for the growth of the soul.

It is natural that huge responsibility comes with mental pressure and stress. Not a single person has been successful in this world without getting stressed. Successful people have to make critical decisions, and they have to work very hard to successfully implement them. They create environments to put themselves under greater stress, and they focus on achieving their goals. They gladly endure stress because they have goals they want to achieve, and they end up utilizing stress as power for success. Depending on your attitude, stress can be powerful energy that drives you into action.

That doesn't mean, however, that you should blindly fulfill your responsibilities without considering the means and methods you employ. The results you achieve with sincerity, using all of your passionate creative energy, are truly brilliant in their value.  Do your best to fulfill your responsibilities, but as much as possible, do so in a way that is good for everyone—for you, your organization, and those with whom you interact. If the work you do helps the entire human race, what could be better than that?

Why do people sometimes lack a sense of responsibility? Usually they don't have an awareness of owning that responsibility. People are unable to accept as "mine" the responsibilities given to them, so they actually think of them as burdensome obligations or a heavy yoke restricting their freedom. They try to get rid of that sense of responsibility and escape from it because they don't feel that the responsibility belongs to them.

To develop a sense of responsibility, you must feel a sense of ownership—for your actions, your contributions, your life. You must stand up and say, "This is my responsibility. It's what I should do and what I must do." This realization becomes stronger when you discover the true meaning of your life. When you feel the spiritual significance of your existence as you contribute to your community and society, your level of commitment to your responsibilities will increase. This awareness is a message from the soul.

Having a sense of responsibility means recognizing that "I am a creator" and believing that you have the power to create reality. It is acknowledging that "I created" the situations I face, my own experience, the results of my work, all these things. There is pride and power here. It's like a painter finishing a painting and then signing it. It is saying, "Genuine article guaranteed," and, "I drew this."

In this sense, responsibility is an attitude different from saying, "It's my fault." If "fault" and "mistakes" come to mind when you hear the word "responsibility," then it's easy for you to be passive and fear taking responsibility. When you proclaim yourself a creator of reality and recognize that you have the power to create reality, you will be able to exhibit commensurate power.

> To develop a sense of responsibility, you must feel a sense of ownership.

Fulfilling your responsibilities is an important part of the Study of Living. Through it, you develop the ability to create what you want in reality. No matter how high a level of enlightenment you may have reached, you cannot realize your purpose in society without social roles and responsibilities.

Whether you are a street cleaner, taxi driver, farmer, policeman, or entrepreneur, your work transmits significance and meaning for the growth of your soul. Your responsibilities should not seem like a burden or obligation, but rather be considered precious opportunities to grow your soul.

Courtesy

Courtesy is the fourth trait needed to achieve growth of the soul. Are you a courteous person? What does this mean to you? Courtesy of the kind we should develop for the growth of the soul has a deeper meaning than *etiquette* or *manners*. True courtesy is not about fixed forms of behavior or social formalities, but an expression of a heart full of love and respect.

Courtesy must arise from the heart naturally; it cannot be forced. It's not about merely doing what appears proper. Instead, the energy of the heart must be contained in the action. The tone of each spoken word, every facial expression, even subtle body movements, reflects a person's true heart and mind. If courtesy is not genuine, others will feel this energy. Likewise, when someone experiences true courtesy from another's heart and soul, they can be truly moved.

Every moment in life demands that we treat others with courtesy. It shows respect for the other person, regardless of their social status. Love and respect expressed in the same way to all people (whether a superior, subordinate, or peer) are courtesy. When you treat others with love and respect, your heart will express itself naturally through your actions. Those who do not show love and respect for others eventually grow cold at heart. While they may show courteous behavior toward others, if the feeling is not genuine, eventually relationships will suffer.

Demonstrating genuine courtesy in one's life lays the foundation for respect from others as well. When we feel love and respect from others, we have a sense of true happiness and fulfillment in life. Respect is not something we "get" from others; rather it must be earned through our daily actions, words, and behavior. When other people are deeply moved by our actions, we inevitably gain respect in their hearts.

If you do not feel love and respect from others in your life, go within and look at your own actions. Are you loving and respecting yourself? Are you behaving with love and respect toward the people around you? Are you communicating with honesty and compassion? Do you genuinely have respect for other people's opinions, needs, and desires, or do you seek to fill your own needs first? In most cases, we must learn to give unconditional love and respect to others before it is given back to us.

Sometimes, we have difficulty communicating with others. In such cases, we often blame the other person before we look to ourselves as the cause of the problem. Perhaps our tone has been offensive, or we have not truly "listened" to the other person's point of view and have been quick to judge. In many cases, it is a good idea to look within ourselves and examine our own character and attitudes if we want to solve communication issues. Even if the other person has also not communicated well, we can only change and control our own behavior at that moment. When we change our own behavior for the better, we often find that those around us also change their behaviors and reactions toward us.

Demonstrating genuine courtesy in one's life lays the foundation for respect from others.

Pride is often a stumbling block on one's path toward the growth of the soul. It is human nature to want to be right, to think that our way is the best way, or that our ideas offer the best solutions. We inevitably make mistakes, but many times our pride makes us reluctant to admit them. People often try to justify themselves, claiming that what they have done is right and refusing to acknowledge their mistakes. But the more we justify ourselves, the farther we get from genuine self-esteem. Increasingly, we begin to resent other people and the environment around us. When we can acknowledge our mistakes and accept responsibility for them, we have a chance to grow and develop. We can find solutions to our problems and rise to a higher level of awareness and acceptance.

Courtesy is not only for people. There is courtesy for heaven and courtesy for earth. Heaven and earth are our cosmic parents because they give life to all things. Just as we are taught to "honor our father and mother" in physical form, we must also honor  the cosmic parents of the universe. Unfortunately, mankind has not shown respect for the environmental world around us. We have polluted our air, contaminated our waters, and paved the earth under our feet. By disrespecting heaven and earth, we have deteriorated our planet and sickened our fellow man. We must regain love and respect for our cosmic parents—the nature in which we live—and extend genuine courtesy to all elements of heaven and earth.

Humanity is part of the cosmic family. All creation is within heaven and earth, but humanity has been given the added responsibility of protecting and caring for our cosmic parents. Humanity suffers when we destroy heaven and earth. Only when we show respect and courtesy toward our cosmic parents can we truly walk the path of the Tao.

Faithfulness

The last of the five character traits necessary for the growth of the soul is *faithfulness*. Faithfulness means remaining true to the words spoken between people, keeping your promises, and doing what you have said you will do.

Korea's ancient scripture, the *Cham Jeon Gye Kyung*, says, "A person with faithfulness should draw near to those who have faithfulness, though he barely knows them, and he should distance himself from those who have no faithfulness, though they are kith or kin."

In all times and places, faithfulness has been an important standard for determining a person's character, and a basic virtue for promoting good personal relationships.

Faithfulness commonly signifies remaining true to commitments or obligations toward others, but true faithfulness begins within. Before you can truly make commitments and be true to others, you must first be true to yourself. This means being true to your pure intentions and the inner voice you had at first. In Korea, pure intentions are called *Choshim* or,

> True faithfulness can only be measured in the most difficult situations.

literally, "first mind." If we are easily influenced by our emotions and desires, it can be difficult or nearly impossible to stay true and loyal to our inner guidance—the voice of our true nature.

True faithfulness can only be measured in the most difficult situations. We respect and cherish those who remain loyal even in difficult circumstances. In ideal conditions, almost anyone can keep a promise. But remaining true in a worst-case scenario, when you're driven to the very brink of frustration, is more challenging. Only when you can hold true to your "first mind" can you truly experience the virtue that is part of the Tao.

Occasionally people are disloyal because of selfish desires. These desires usually arise from our basic human needs for security, recognition, and control. It's easy to abandon loyalty when we are mired deeply in any one of these three needs.

Faithfulness can be found not only in relationships between human beings, but in relationships between humans and nature, and even within the natural world itself. Faithfulness is a principle of transactions. Transactions happen ceaselessly in the natural world and in the rest of the cosmos. For example, after it rains, the water on the ground evaporates and the water vapor again becomes rain, which wets the ground once more. A sapling sprouts from the ground in the springtime and in the fall its leaves drop, returning to the ground. Everything is a transaction, a give-and-take in accordance with the natural laws of energy and the Tao.

Faithfulness is a mindset of trusting and remaining true to the laws of the Tao. It's not about the good and evil, profit and loss, wealth and poverty, or laughing and crying that happen in the visible, phenomenal world, but about understanding and following the laws of the world of energy—the invisible world of the Tao. Knowing the path that the soul must follow and deciding to follow that path, this is the original mind, the first mind. That's why the big obstacle to the growth of the soul is losing faithfulness, not remaining true to that first pure mind that you had for your soul.

Your soul must become pure enough to remain loyal. Purifying your soul means the character of your Ki energy becomes clearer. That is why we engage in energy training for the growth of our soul—to increase our faithfulness to our chosen path and to become one with the Tao.

This applies not only to faithfulness, but also to honesty, sincerity, responsibility, and courtesy, the other character traits needed for the growth of the soul. Development of such traits requires a change of energy through training; it can't be done through thinking, knowledge, or faith. In other words, we must change the character of our Ki.

The reason we lose such traits is that we readily give up our hearts to the voices of our minds and demands of our bodies. Selfishness and the ego arise out of the body. If we comply with the desires and attachments that are created by that selfishness and ego, it is difficult for us to develop good character.

To recover and develop these five characteristics, we must pursue our interest in spiritual awakening and growth earnestly and ceaselessly. Open your Tao eyes and walk toward the completion of your soul, going with the waves of life energy. The ferry boat that transports our souls is Ki energy, and the lighthouse that illuminates our path is the light of our divine nature.

How beautiful and precious is the work of developing character? The five character traits are like five kinds of jewels embroidered in the cloth of your soul. The colors and shapes of those jewels may differ, but they have all come out of your true nature. Allow those five traits to shine like brilliant gemstones. Their light will illuminate your life, and the lives of others, as well.

CHAPTER EIGHT

The Evolution of Love

IT IS OFTEN SAID that human beings are "born to love." But what does this actually mean? Have you ever really considered what love is? We use the term in many different ways to describe a variety of relationships ranging from romantic love, to familial love, to friendly love, and more. So what is this intense emotion that can leave the human heart bursting with joy and feeling immensely full one minute, and painfully bruised and wounded the next? Have you ever defined love for yourself? What is the first thing that comes to your mind when you think of this powerful, four-letter word?

A red heart is typically used to symbolize love. It also symbolizes the life-giving, beating organ that pumps oxygenated blood throughout your body. People often associate the emotion of love as arising in the heart, even though the brain plays the primary role in love.

When we feel love, especially romantic love, our heartbeat quickens. Viewed physiologically, the sympathetic nervous system is excited by the neurotransmitters secreted in the brain, and this elevates the heart rate. When we experience a quickening in our hearts because of intense emotion, passion, or other stimuli, we often associate the feeling we experience as the sensation of "being alive." This is why many people will often say that the first time they felt alive was when they were in love.

Love has been related to the heart in almost every culture. The Ancient Egyptians placed great importance on the preservation of the body because they believed that it housed the "spirit" for the afterlife. They considered the heart to be the most powerful part of a person because it was believed to be the seat of the soul and of love, or the center of the person's being and intelligence. During the process of mummification, the heart was preserved and left inside the body while other key organs—the stomach, liver, lungs, and intestines—were removed and stored separately in special jars. Meanwhile, the brain was removed and destroyed because the Egyptians did not understand the importance of the brain.

In Traditional Chinese Medicine the heart is considered to be the "seat of the mind," and its highest expression is love. The heart is associated with the fire element, which emotionally correlates with the mind and its stability. Enthusiasm, warmth in human relationships, and conscious awareness all reside in the heart.

> Developing a compassionate heart is the hallmark of the True Self.

The heart is also associated with the fourth chakra, the center of the chakra system. It serves as a wellspring of love and compassion and a gateway to healing. It is the seat of all emotional experience and the integrator of opposites in the human psyche: mind and body, male and female, persona and shadow, ego and unity. The health of our fourth chakra is dependent on the health of our minds and emotions. When this chakra is open and balanced we feel joy and love, when closed and imbalanced, we experience sadness and anger.

Compassion has been described as the highest virtue, or the highest Ki, which is expressed through the heart chakra. When this center is opened, we face the world with an open mind and loving heart. From here, we can develop a beautiful character based on personal integrity and ethical conduct. We can reach out beyond the egoic mind and experience connection and oneness with others. Developing a compassionate heart is the hallmark of the True Self.

If I were to describe love in terms of energy, I would say that love is experienced as "waves of energy from the fourth chakra, created by a true heart." A "true heart" activates the energy system of the fourth chakra and creates waves. These waves are detected within us as feelings and emotions. When I direct my attention toward another person with an open heart, my true heart creates energy waves that the other person can feel. Likewise, the heart energy directed at me by someone else can also be felt. When both of us are communicating with our true hearts, our energy waves resonate with one another and grow even stronger.

The fourth chakra holds two kinds of energy. One is the pure energy of the soul; the other, the energy of emotion created by desire. Depending on which of the two energies we use, we have the capability to experience soul love or emotional love. If the physical energy of desire and emotion are prevalent, we call it emotional love; if compassion and unconditional love are being expressed by our True Self, we call it soul love.

Commonly, when we hear the word "love," we often think of romantic, physical love between two people. Most of our cultural expressions of love, from pop songs and TV dramas to movies and other art forms, focus on the theme of love between the sexes. But true love is not only expressed in a romantic sense. A true heart can exist in any human relationship. It can reflect the love between parents and children, teachers and students, friends and peers, and between colleagues at work.

Though it is difficult to quantify or measure, love is often described in terms of varying degrees. We refer to friendly love, romantic love, brotherly love, unconditional love, and more. Most of us have experienced conditional love during our lifetime. It is the expression of love that is most common in ordinary human relationships because it is based on the ego's desires and attachments.

It is also offered as a kind of reward for doing what others want us to do, for acting in ways we think we should behave, or is based on a give-and-take expression. The giver of this form of love always expects something in return. Conditional love is the cause of most of the challenges and pain that we experience in our relationships.

A grander, more encompassing kind of love is unconditional love. It represents the soul love that is freely given by our True Self. This love expects nothing in return. It is synonymous with the compassion, or the highest form of Ki, that we spoke of earlier. This love has no boundaries and no limits. It cannot be contained by anything, and it can encompass everything—the people around you, organizations, the earth, and even the entire universe. Our ability to express this kind of limitless love grows as our hearts and minds expand because of our increasing levels of consciousness.

> Our ability to express limitless love grows as our hearts and minds expand.

In Asian culture, the evolution of love can be divided generally into three stages according to the object loved and to the growth of one's consciousness. These three levels of love are called: *Hyo*, true love for one's parents; *Choong*, true love for one's country or organization; and Tao, true love for humanity and the universe. As the scale of the object loved gradually grows from the individual, to an organization, to the cosmos, the scale of one's consciousness grows, too. That is why I call this the "evolution of love." Let us look at each of these three types of love.

Hyo, Love for Individuals

The first stage in the evolution of love is that which we feel for individuals. It is expressed as *Hyo*. Actually, the precise meaning of Hyo is the duty of children to serve their parents. The character Hyo (孝) combines the character *No* (老), which means the elderly, with the character *Ja* (子), which means offspring, to show a child helping and serving his or her parents. In modern terms, it means children loving and caring for their parents. Hyo is a natural expression of gratitude and repayment for the noble kindness and dedication parents show in giving birth to and raising their children. It is not a sense of obligation.

In Germany they have a saying: "A father more willingly maintains ten sons, than ten sons will maintain one father." This proverb describes the immense love and commitment that parents often have for their children. A parent's love is so great that it is not ever likely to be repaid.

What, then, is the best way to practice Hyo? Is it to provide material support such as expensive gifts or sumptuous feasts? Does this mean that a poor person cannot practice Hyo? Is it familial support provided from a sense of obligation? No. Zhuangzi, an influential Chinese philosopher who lived around the 4th century BCE, once said, "To be filial out of support is easy; to be filial out of love is hard." This quote reflects the true nature of Hyo in that it must come from a true and benevolent heart. Hyo does not mean simply to support one's parents materially; rather it is the expression of spiritual oneness and gratitude that comes from a genuine and unconditionally loving heart.

In Asia it is said that Hyo is the basis of a hundred kinds of behavior, the foundation of ten thousand kinds of learning. From the foundation of Hyo for one's parents may spring many things such as brotherly love, friendship, camaraderie, affection, or even intimacy. Eventually, if you practice Hyo toward your nation the way you do toward your parents, it becomes Choong; if you practice Hyo toward your cosmic parents—heaven and earth—it becomes the Tao.

In the Analects of Confucius, it is written, "Being truly filial to one's parents and reflecting brotherly love in the affairs of state is practicing good government." In essence, this means that the heart that practices Hyo develops and grows the principles of a good leader or ruler. In the Canon of Filial Piety, a compilation of questions and answers on Hyo between Confucius and his disciple, Tseng-tzu, it is written, "When we have established our character by the practice of the Tao so as to make our name famous in future ages and thereby glorify our parents, this is the end of filial piety." They saw the culmination of Hyo as not only respecting one's parents, but also as practicing the Tao in such a manner that one's name and character would be so great as to ultimately glorify them.

> Hyo is the expression of gratitude that comes from a genuine loving heart.

What is the state of Hyo in modern society? Do you think that genuine Hyo exists? Before discussing this further, should we take a look at the state of the family in today's society? In one opinion survey, when asked what they valued most, the preponderance of respondents said "family." This means that they placed great importance on their family members and often equated it to happiness. But when asked, "Is your family happy?" how many people can readily answer "Yes"?

One of the biggest problems of our society today is that the family unit is breaking down and disintegrating. Families reflect the societal trends of the times. According to the Population Reference Bureau, economic and social trends in the United States since the year 2000 have been marked by violence and terrorism, severe economic recession, a housing meltdown, high unemployment, loss of household wealth, increased migration and immigration, declining educational attainment, and greater disparity between the wealthy and the poor. These conditions cause increased marital discord and divorce rates; more childhood runaways and family violence; higher educational dropout and juvenile delinquency; staggering community crime rates; and even more suicides.

Ideas through which people view themselves and the world become deep-rooted in childhood. Unhappiness at home directly leads to unhappiness for the children, and that unhappiness expands into societal problems. Also, as dialogue between family members is cut off and spiritual solidarity weakened, parents fail to serve as good examples for their children, and they are unable to teach them the solid values necessary for creating an enlightened, compassionate society.

In Korea, there's a saying, "Parents must become wholly filial if their children are to become halfway filial." Filial and fraternal love must first be learned at home. We have forgotten that the family is the most basic unit for the development and practice of good character, where compassion, honesty, sincerity, empathy, gratitude, and love must first be learned.

The family unit is a small training ground where members gather for the growth of their own souls, as well as for one another. If we viewed the family from this perspective, then our standards would change and we would become more prudent—beginning with our choice of the person we marry. Rather than using standards such as material wealth, good looks, or social power, we would choose a spouse who is honest, sincere, and responsible, and who could be a partner for mutual growth. Our educational system would begin with the basic character and duties of a good human being, rather than competitiveness, material wealth, and gaining power over others.

Choong, Love for Causes

The next evolution of love, beyond that of Hyo, is love for an organization or group, called *Choong*. In Korea, mentioning Choong, or "loyalty," first brings to mind love for one's country. It signifies the love of an individual for the organization to which he belongs, such as a company, community, or other group association. The character Choong (忠) combines the character *Jung* (中), meaning "center," with the

> Choong is the spontaneous dedication that arises from the heart in pursuit of a great cause.

character *Shim* (心), meaning "heart" or "mind." Choong could be interpreted to mean "the mind's center." Choong is not a political concept, but the spontaneous and practical dedication that arises from the heart in pursuit of a great cause.

When a person understands loyalty and has a sense of mission, we say that his consciousness has evolved. In Korean society, Choong is the basic standard for gaining trust and recognition within an organization. Genuine Choong is not about being loyal to your organization only when it is good to you, but rather, it means remaining true to the very end, no matter what situation may arise.

One of the most respected figures in Korean history was General Lee Soonshin, a naval commander noted for his victories against the Japanese navy during its invasions of Korea (1592-1598) during the Joseon Dynasty.

During the Battle of Myeongnyang, General Lee Soonshin victoriously led a fleet of only 13 ships against an enemy of 333 vessels. He is considered a symbol of Choong not only because he successfully led an extremely inferior military force in good order and, through preparation and superior tactics, was virtually undefeated, but also because he remained true to Choong during circumstances in which it was truly difficult to be loyal. He was a victim of plots by people jealous of his achievements, was dismissed and imprisoned three times, and was twice forced to serve in the military as a commoner of no rank. He had more public support than the King and was therefore suspected of making himself ruler one day. Despite this situation, he dedicated himself to defending his country and its people from foreign invaders. He ultimately fulfilled his mission and died in battle.

Countries have a national center, companies have a corporate center, and religions have a religious center. No matter what your organization, it is bound to have a centripetal point. An organization can function smoothly when its members focus and direct their minds and hearts toward its center. And when an organization functions smoothly, its members will benefit. This is called the "Principle of Centripetal Force and Centrifugal Force."

Imagine that you're moving your hand in a circle, which holds a foot-long rubber band with a weight attached to the other end of it. The power of the hand spinning the rubber band creates the centripetal force, and the circular movement of the weight creates the centrifugal force. The greater the centripetal force, the stronger the centrifugal force. What would happen, though, if the centripetal force disappeared? If you let go of the rubber band, the circular motion of the weight would cease. In this way, centrifugal force can appear only when centripetal force exists. Conversely, what would happen if, while you were spinning the weight, the rubber band broke because you spun it too forcefully? The rubber band could no longer move in a great circle, no matter how much you spun it, because there would be no weight attached, and its power would weaken. In this way, centripetal force can only appear when centrifugal force exists.

> An organization can function smoothly when its members direct their minds toward its center.

You can also witness this principle when you apply it to a company, organization, or country to which you belong. When you and other like-minded individuals are focused around the central purpose or mission of a particular organization, company, or country, everyone is able to be active within its boundaries and sphere of influence. Everyone contributes to a shared vision, and all are strengthened and benefit.

But if the members, driven by ego and selfish desires, seek to pursue their individual goals and broaden their domain in a way that is counterproductive to the vision and needs of the group, the organization begins to weaken and ultimately fails. It is similar to a cancer cell that begins to multiply unchecked; eventually it kills its host and thereby itself at the same time. Similarly, people who lack the consciousness to work for the betterment of the whole are often considered by others to be self-centered.

The difference between evolved consciousness and ego is simple: each has a different center. The ego is self-centered. It is driven by its own desires and attachments, by its physical form and delusions of the mind. Conversely, evolved consciousness is centered on the bigger picture, the whole of which it is a part.

There is something we must point out here. When we hear the words "centered in the whole," people sometimes think this consciousness focuses solely on others, ignoring the being that is itself. This interpretation comes out of a dichotomous perspective that views the self and the whole as different entities. Those whose consciousness is evolved know that they, as individuals, do not exist separately from the whole, but that they are the whole and the whole is them. The sphere of their consciousness expands, like ripples in a pond stirred up by a falling drop of water. They can see the small ripple (their self) and understand how their actions expand into larger ripples, affecting the larger whole. They are one in the same.

When we talk about being "centered in the whole," there may be various kinds of "whole." On a small scale, the "it" could be the company or community to which you belong, and on a larger scale it could be a nation, the entire human race, or even the whole planet. The sphere of your consciousness expands and evolves to the size of the object you can embrace. Depending on where it is centered, your consciousness can expand or shrink without limit. Where are you placing your center?

Conflict Among
Different Levels of Love

What, then, is the greatest center in our world? By this I mean, what is a center that can be shared by the entire human race and all the living organisms on the earth? It is the earth itself. Going further, it is the universe to which the earth belongs. Individual consciousness expanding to the extent that it contains the earth and the cosmos is Tao-level consciousness. Anyone can go beyond Hyo, transcend Choong, and reach the level of Tao when his or her human consciousness expands.

Why is it so difficult for human consciousness to experience Tao-level consciousness? It is because Hyo, Choong, and Tao conflict and struggle with one another at times, binding human consciousness. Though you may travel the path of the Tao, Hyo blocks you and Choong stands in your way.

First, let us look at how Hyo and Choong conflict. Let's say that a young person is sincere, capable, and smart, so his parents expect him to get a good job and become financially successful. But instead of choosing a stable, comfortable life, this person enlists in the military to fight for his country, or joins a movement to protect the environment. How many parents could really say, "Well done! I'm proud of you."? What would you tell your child if you were in this situation?

> Hyo, Choong, and Tao often conflict and struggle with one another.

Most parents would probably admit that they would want to dissuade their child. "Those are good aspirations, but they're for others to do, not you," they might say. Some parents might say, "Patriotism? Environmentalism? Family is more important. I've dedicated my life to raising you. You must be successful and fulfill my hopes for you." In these circumstances, it is often difficult for a child to know which path to choose. If he engages in Choong, Hyo is disappointed; if in Hyo, Choong is disappointed.

A similar conflict exists between Choong and Tao. When the

representatives of a state meet in their national assembly to decide on policy without any recognition of the principles of Tao, they argue about whether the policy coincides with the interests of their own political party before they even consider whether it is in the best interest of their country's citizens.

At the 2009 United Nations Climate Change Conference, held in Copenhagen, Denmark, officials from 192 countries gathered to establish an ambitious global climate agreement for the period beginning in 2012 when the first commitment period under the Kyoto Protocol would expire. The conference was unable to reach a binding agreement for long-term action because representatives placed the interests of their own countries first, rather than what action would serve the human race as a whole. This is a clear example of the confrontation between Choong and Tao.

Similar confrontations exist when applied to religions views. Religions ought to practice and serve as examples of great Tao love, but excessive loyalty among believers for the faith to which they belong stands in the way of peace for all humanity. Even after resolving to cooperate and respect one another's views for world peace, many people still believe that their religion is the only one that can save human souls. Interreligious conflict will never be resolved until believers abandon their obstinate insistence that their religion alone is the best.

Despite the face that the development of Choong toward the greater Tao is the way to promote greater coexistence on the planet, the reality of the human race is that it fails to live up to this. Not only is Choong blocking the path to Tao, but even different forms of Choong stand in the way of one another in mutual confrontation. On a small scale, such confrontations evolve from the group selfishness that arises when believers trust in the superiority of the groups to which they belong, and ignore or despise other groups. On a larger scale, ethnic groups conflict with one another over land uses, religious zealots kill believers of other faiths, and nations go to war.

The history of the human race has been marked by numerous wars, and the 20th century has been particularly marked by war and violence. Political and religious leaders have always had their justifications for war, usually couched in waging "war for peace," freedom, democracy, or the justice of the members of the groups they are inciting. In most cases, however, their "peace" was only benefiting the small group to which they belonged, and not all of mankind.

What has most reasonably justified bloodshed in human history is war. If an individual kills another person, it is murder, but if he kills someone as part of a group in a battle, then he is praised for his courage and bravery. Moreover, battles between religions are glorified in the name of "holy war," which is said to be carrying out the "will of God." Our world has become a battleground between countless beliefs, values, and bits of information called "Gods" that have been created by human beings. They all cry out for peace, justice, and love,

> Our world has become a battleground between bits of information called "Gods."

but most are preoccupied with territorial battles. Even now, people raise their voices talking about love, only to mercilessly trample those who do not agree with their views. We have yet to learn tolerance and master coexistence.

So Choong confronts Choong. The end result is that people assign the term "loyalty" to group selfishness, manipulated for the benefit of certain privileged classes. Genuine loyalty, or Choong, must be linked with the Tao. Choong cannot resolve the problems caused by Choong. Unless the human race begins to compromise, coexist, and live in harmony, the Global Village will be nothing but an empty dream. The only way to resolve the conflicts and confrontations between different forms of Choong is to expand our consciousness into Tao love.

Tao Consciousness

The Tao is not something that belongs to something else, nor can it be. For the Tao is the great life force of the cosmos itself: the principle of nature through which all things are created and destroyed, come together and disperse. The law of nature is just there; it is the life energy of the cosmos coming into being. The law of the great life force of the cosmos cannot be owned or dominated by anyone, nor can it be defied. Just as when winter passes, spring comes, flowers bloom, and birds sing, just as the moon rises when the sun sets and the sun rises when the moon sets, the never-ending cycle of energy's action is the Tao.

The highest evolution of love is Tao love, love for the cosmos. It is the recognition that we are all one, various representations of the Universal life force energy that is everything and yet nothing. When we talk about "the cosmos," we don't mean the spaces of the universe embroidered by countless planets and galaxies. We are referring to the natural laws of the universe, which animate everything in the world around us. There is no need to go into deep outer space. You can discover the principles of life just by observing the natural world around you, by tuning in to your own breath, or even by feeling your heart beat within your own body. Tao is simply the movement of life energy dwelling in all things in creation.

How, then, can you apply Tao consciousness in your daily life? First, we need a centripetal center, a center of consciousness able to resolve conflicts between different forms of loyalty (Choong) and able to unite as one the consciousness of the whole human race! What could it be?

The greatest physical object through which we can practice Tao consciousness is the earth itself. Every human being on earth is a soul companion journeying at the same time and sharing the goal of the growth and completion of our souls. By examining how an individual human's or organization's activities—in their individual lives, academics, economics, science, religion, or politics—contribute to the vitality and sustainability of the earth and the existence of our fellow beings, we can determine the level of a person's or organization's consciousness. If we're interested only in our own vitality, or the vitality of the organizations to which we belong, then it is clear that our consciousness is self-centered and still governed by our ego. When we place the vitality of the planet upon which we live at the forefront of our actions, we are beginning to practice Tao consciousness.

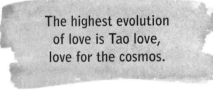

The highest evolution of love is Tao love, love for the cosmos.

Expressed differently, Tao consciousness is earth consciousness. It is demonstrated when we put the earth at the center of our actions. Placing the earth at the center of all human values is the key for creating an enlightened society and achieving world peace. If we place a religion or a country at the center, then we cannot help fighting each other. We must now shift our center. Just as the life of the earth can be maintained only if it orbits the sun, so, too, the life of the human race can be maintained only when we put the earth at the center of our lives.

When we view our existence as centered around the earth, we can more openly perceive where conflicts between countries, eth-nicities, and religions begin and seek better ways to solve those conflicts. To say that we should put the earth at the center of our values is not to say that we should have faith in our planet. What we are saying is that we should view the earth as the living organism it is, and we should make the well-being of this organism and its people our top priority. A community of true harmony and coexistence will finally be born when we all recognize the earth as our core value and begin to respect one another from a position of equality.

In a material way, these times are evolving into the Age of the Global Village. We can send, receive, and exchange information beyond the borders of countries through developed information and transportation technologies, without being limited to a single region or nation. A new world is truly coming. But has a genuine Global Village truly come to pass? I contend that it has not. While we enjoy numerous benefits achieved through technological advancement, individual and group selfishness continue to exist as solid, unseen barriers.

This is why Hyo and Choong must change into Tao. In earlier times, when your village was the whole world and all you had to do was live happily with your family and neighbors, Hyo alone was enough. During times when people moved by foot or on horseback, limiting their world view to just what was over the next ridge was enough. As modes of transportation evolved and people's fields of vision grew wider, they came to learn that people of different colors, beliefs, faiths, and even nationalities existed. People's worldviews expanded into Choong, group-centered consciousness. For a time, Hyo and Choong consciousness were enough for someone to be considered moral and good. Now many of us are realizing that the time has come to evolve into an even wider view.

As we embark into the 21st century, you can have coffee and a pastry at a New York bakery in the morning, drink wine at a restaurant in Italy for dinner, and enjoy the sunrise in Hong Kong the next day. You can even globetrot around the world via the Internet while you sit comfortably in your own home. Wherever you want to go, whatever you want to know, you can find the information by surfing the Web or by video chatting in real time. People worldwide can simultaneously watch live telecasts of the Olympics or champion matches at the World Cup. And in the United States of America, people of all races and nationalities come together to mix, mingle, and live together. Today people change their nationalities and intermarry with other races so that the concepts of "nation" and "ethnic group" have grown harder to define.

> A community of true harmony will be born when we all recognize the earth as our core value.

The world has already gone far beyond the dimensions of Hyo and Choong. The times when we were attached to one nation or religion have passed. We cannot usher in a genuine Age of the Global Village unless the level of our collective consciousness evolves. This is the Tao consciousness. It is not enough to have a few masters or gurus who have awakened to Tao consciousness; everyone must now become an enlightened master.

We now must tear down the boundaries separating Hyo, Choong, and Tao and unite them as one. Love your family to your heart's content (Hyo) and be loyal to the causes you serve through

Choong; yet link these virtues with love for the whole (Tao) and peace for the human race will follow. This is the vision that I see—an open society in which Hyo, Choong, and Tao flow freely within Tao consciousness. Individuals stand hand-in-hand; nations shoulder-to-shoulder; religions open-hearted as one; all for the sake of their common value, their common center, the earth.

How do we move toward this Tao consciousness? We must dissolve the ego. Genuine truth must take center stage in that place from which the ego has vanished. We must understand that there is something more precious than individual and group ego. If you have in your possession some gold, and someone proposes to give you something else in exchange for your gold, you would first ask what that something was. If that something were silver or bronze, then you would not hand over your gold, but if it were diamonds, you would readily give your gold away. In the same way, you must discard your ego and choose truth when you understand that truth is more precious than the ego. You exchange Hyo for Choong, and Choong for Tao, and ultimately you realize that both Hyo and Choong arise out of Tao.

One misunderstanding people have is that discarding the ego means abandoning themselves for some external object. That is not the case at all. To discard the ego means to discard the small self. We come to realize that a Greater Self can be found in its place. The Greater Self is the spiritual energy body and the essence of who I am, not the me that is limited by the ego or by my physical body. It is the realization that this is the great life force of the universe itself.

What can each of us do to abandon our egos and allow our consciousness to expand toward Tao consciousness? We must awaken. Hyo and Choong can be realized to some degree by anyone leading a regular life with a normal view of the world. Tao consciousness, however, must be diligently studied and pursued through daily practice and awakened living.

Awakening to and practicing Tao consciousness is not just an ideal. It is knowing that the universal life energy is the essense of Tao and experiencing this energy through your body. In other words, awakening to Tao consciousness means bringing to completion the energy system in the human body. It also means using your own life energy, to which you have awakened, to contribute to the vital activity of the whole, and to amplify the life energy field of the whole. We must have genuine power in order to practice Tao. That power comes from your energy centers, the Dahnjons. Physical power arises out of the lower Dahnjon; the power of love comes out of the middle Dahnjon; and the power of the spirit comes out of the upper Dahnjon. You change your surroundings and the world with that power.

> Tear down the boundaries separating Hyo, Choong, and Tao and unite them as one.

The Tao is inevitably about nothing more than flowery words and unrealizable ideas for people whose Dahnjons are weak, because they lack the drive to put their thoughts into action. They need practices for developing the power of their Dahnjons to unify their thoughts, words, and deeds. That is why *The Great Learning*, which is one of the Seven Chinese Classics, describes the process of human moral and spiritual development in this way: *Sooshin* (One must first cultivate one's body and mind), *Jega* (then one can manage one's family), *Chigook* (contribute to one's organization or nation), and *Pyungchunha* (and bring peace to the world).

Contributing one's family is Hyo, to one's organization and nation is Choong, and to the world is Tao. But, before engaging in Hyo, Choong, and Tao, we must first cultivate our bodies and minds. It is important to develop character and practice the love of Hyo, Choong, and Tao through the Study of Practice and the Study of Living so that Hyo, Choong, and Tao do not remain mere concepts.

If you have understood the three stages in the evolution of love—Hyo, Choong, and Tao—then it means that you know life and that you know humanity. It is the path to big love, not to being bound and attached to small love. All have within their hearts a desire to practice big love. They are lonely and sad because, although their hearts are filled with love, they are not able to express that love adequately.

Love from your heart. Allow love to flow from your heart, like the pure, clear waters of a rushing stream. Standing water putrefies and gives off a foul odor. In the same way, selective, closed love fills your heart with frustration. Love from the heart is unconditional love, an open thing that is offered widely and freely. When our hearts revive, we cannot help but love with a great love, for we feel all living things connected with ourselves and the light, sound, and waves of life they emit appear so beautiful to us.

CHAPTER NINE

Three Realizations
to the Tao

AT THIS MOMENT, OVER SEVEN BILLION PEOPLE live on planet Earth. It is said that approximately one hundred billion people have lived and died throughout human history. Can you picture a crowd of one hundred billion people? Every day, approximately 350,000 people are born and 150,000 die. That means that every second, somewhere on the planet, four people are born and two people die.

What caused all of this human life? Given the scope of humanity, have you ever wondered if your personal existence has any meaning? Have you contemplated the question, "Why am I here and what is my true purpose in life?" This is the ultimate question of the Tao and one you should ask repeatedly.

In the course of studying this question, there are three important realizations that are inherent in life on earth. Through these three realizations, you will obtain answers to your questions about the Tao and draw much closer to the Tao.

First Realization: Suffering

The first realization is that life is suffering. Of course, there are moments of happiness and beauty, periods when we are like a flower in full bloom. Even so, life is marked by unwanted accidents and adversity.

Basically, we all have to look after our bodies while we live. And the demands and complaints of our bodies are endless. We have to eat when our bodies are hungry, sleep when they're tired, clothe them when they're cold, and wash them when they're sweaty. And that is not all. Countless diseases—ailments of the eyes, nose, mouth, legs, and our internal organs—lie in wait at every turn; if we're even a little negligent in how we manage them, our bodies howl in pain. Beginning with getting up in the morning, washing, and eating, who knows how many hours we invest each day in taking care of and leading our bodies about? We have to continually earn money to satisfy the body's desires and basic needs: food, clothing, and sleep. While we are busy providing these things, life passes us by.

The body is not the only thing that gives us pain. If we look at it a certain way, our mental pain can be even greater. We live in the clutches of comparative consciousness and compulsions, which forces us to try to be better than others in order to make it in the competition of survival for possession and control. Our brains are being abused by doubt and fear of others, and by our own feelings of inferiority. Much

> Understanding life's suffering allows you to meet difficulty and challenges with more acceptance and grace.

of the pain we suffer results from identifying ourselves with our egos. The ego relentlessly seeks to possess, to get recognition, and to control. We feel pain unless those needs are satisfied. When we have the power to separate ourselves from our egos and watch ourselves, we can reduce needless pain.

This does not mean, however, that we can completely avoid the suffering of life. In the larger sense, life's suffering encompasses more than physical or mental pain. It includes all the limitations that come from existing in an imperfect physical state in an imperfect world. We have hopes, dreams, and good intentions that often go unrealized. We have moments of happiness and joy but, like stars that glitter and then fade in the night sky, they don't last forever. We have loved ones, friends, and other relationships that eventually change or disappear. And we never know when our time will come, or what the next day will bring. This uncertainty of existence is another unavoidable part of life.

I have met many people who don't like to hear that life is suffering, who feel resistance to such comments. In particular, people accustomed to a culture that stresses achievement, challenge, and positive thinking seem to think that this statement is too negative. It is not intended, however, as a form of pessimism that stresses the tragedy of life. It is not meant to suggest that we should avoid joy and happiness in life. Rather, it is simply a matter of acknowledging the universal truth that suffering is inevitable because we are finite, imperfect life forms. It means serenely accepting that suffering is a part of life.

Who actually lives a more meaningful life, the person who accepts suffering as inevitable or the person who denies its reality? When we taste the bitterness of life, we come to understand it more deeply. Those who realize that life inevitably includes difficulty are less stressed, even when they experience painful events. They are better able to deal with life's challenges in a calm, patient, and courageous manner. When good things happen, they relish those precious events with complete gratitude. They also have more compassion and understanding for others who suffer amid life's pain.

Conversely, those who believe that life must be perfect and full of joy inevitably have a much more narrow view of life and the world. They are stressed by even trivial challenges, which thus obstruct their own happiness and desires. Instead of accepting such things as a part of life and learning from them, when confronted by unfortunate events they easily give in to anger or frustration. They become resentful because they believe the world and the people around them are the cause of their misfortune. Those who fail to accept the universal law of suffering lack compassion and empathy. When we accept suffering as a part of life, we become more humble and truthful.

Life is nothing more than a succession of painful experiences that are attenuated by flickering moments of happiness. Opening to this awareness is critically important to the path of Tao. Those who truly and deeply realize that life is suffering do not remain at that stage. "Is life truly suffering, and is the essence of life really nothing more than this? Clearly, there must be some way to escape from this suffering," they think, and set out on a continuous journey in search of that

> When we accept suffering as a part of life, we become more humble and truthful.

something that will relieve their distress. The suffering of life, approached with an awakened consciousness, can be a spiritual guide more wonderful than any other and a shortcut to the Tao.

Second Realization: Transience

The second realization to the Tao is that all things change. This is called *transience*. It means that nothing ever stays the same. Everything that exists changes. Our physical bodies change, our emotions change, our society changes, the earth changes, and even the universe changes.

Take a look back at your life. There was a time when you were a toddler with a runny nose, and a time in your youth when you were full of dreams and curiosity about the world. Time flew by and one day, you looked at who you had become. Gone was your youthful exuberance, your taut skin, your toned body. Perhaps you were still attractive, filled with curiosity and visions of the future, but in a different way.

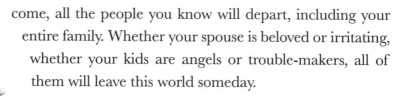

How will you have changed in another ten years? Will you still be here? We all leave this world sooner or later. When their times come, all the people you know will depart, including your entire family. Whether your spouse is beloved or irritating, whether your kids are angels or trouble-makers, all of them will leave this world someday.

How will the world around you have changed? Not just individuals, but entire societies and natural ecosystems are ever-changing. Conventional wisdom, beliefs, cultures, and customs that were once thought to be completely obvious change as people's consciousness changes. The abolition of the long-accepted institution of slavery, the recognition of a woman's right to participate fully in society, and recent legalization of homosexual marriage are noticeable examples of this.

The natural environment is in a constant state of change. As the planet lives, breathes, and transforms itself, dynamic forces and powerful energies are constantly at work. The earth never rests: over billions of years, the earth experiences geological changes, climatic shifts, evolution, appearances and disappearances of entire species. Even the sun, moon, stars and entire universe are transmuting themselves from moment to moment.

Transience is the most universal law of all phenomena. More precisely, change is essential to existence. Similar to the way a bicycle keeps from falling over by rolling along, there can be neither phenomena nor existence without change. This is not something that you can realize only through hard research and study; the law of transience can be observed in the entire nature of the extant world.

When we truly recognize the transient nature of life, we inevitably become more humble. We come to acknowledge this fact, and say to ourselves, "Yeah, no matter how proud and confident I act, I am one little soul struggling with the suffering and impermanence of life." When we see ourselves as one of many who share in suffering, we no longer resent or look down on others. Because we know that everyone is doing his or her best to figure out how to be happy and live in a difficult situation, we begin to have more compassion, more respect, and more grace with the world around us.

Even though we feel, in each twist and turn of life, that life isn't permanent, many people nevertheless struggle against the impermanence of human existence. Why? Perhaps because of the feeling of emptiness that arises within us when we are faced with the reality of constant change. If life is transient, what can we hold on to? How can we ever feel secure? What is the meaning of it all? If I am so insignificant, how can I live a life of significance?

> When we awaken to the reality of transience, we are liberated from the suffering that comes from attachment.

We try hard to turn away from the truth of transience because it causes a feeling of emptiness within us. The reality of the immense cosmos is difficult to bear, so we don't want to look at it. We work hard to turn away from the truth of impermanence and try to forget the empty feeling that the finiteness of our existence gives us. We don't want to awaken from our delusion and fantasy, so we continue to pretend that everything will continue to exist as it is, changeless.

There is an important delusion that keeps even people who have awakened to this fact from really escaping from it. Some think that, although everything *else* changes and is impermanent, they themselves are an exception to that transience. Even though they accept that everything else appears and disappears, they mistakenly believe that their own existence is eternal. Transience is just a fact of life. We cannot attach to it any reason, feeling, or excuse. We ourselves change, and the objects to which we are attached also change.

If we think that we are an exception to impermanence, from that moment on our battle with transience causes much suffering. Because we are under the illusion that we are forever changeless, we want other things connected with us to last forever, too. We will fall into even greater attachment and suffering because of our deluded grasping, thinking that what we have will last forever. Ultimately, we cannot escape losing everything when we die. When we deny this, we drive our lives into pain and suffering. All of our attachments are actually futile because there is nothing there for us to grasp, nothing we can actually hold on to. When we awaken to the reality of transience, we are liberated from the suffering that comes from attachment.

Understanding the transient nature of life is actually a great comfort. If we accept that everything changes, our inherent clinging to attachments and desires vanishes. Herein is the answer and end to our suffering. We won't seek to control other people, places, things, or events. Suddenly we can go with the ebb and flow of life and ride its smooth or turbulent currents. Our motto more readily becomes, "This too shall pass." When we understand the law of transience, we face life with an openness and acceptance of all that is in the here and now.

Third Realization:
Selflessness (Muah)

The key to the third realization to the Tao is the question, "Who am I?" What is the first thing that comes to your mind when you ask this question? Your name? Your face? Your social title? The best answer that our rational mind might give is, "I don't really know."

There are so many ways we define ourselves: "I am somebody's husband and somebody's father." "I am somebody's wife." "I am someone's daughter or son; someone's friend." "I am someone who has a certain position at some company." "I'm a student at a certain school."

Ironically, your name and the social tags attached to your name may pose the greatest obstacles to genuinely answering this question. You, whom you think of as yourself now, are an accumulation of information formed through various experiences. Your name, age, occupation, memories, likes and dislikes, successes and failures, strengths and weaknesses, and dreams and aspirations are just bits of information that have come together to form your self-image. Although these information bits do indeed influence who you are, they are not *actually you*.

> You, whom you think of as yourself now, are an accumulation of information.

The bits of information that create the image that is "you" are not fixed. They change constantly. In one moment you might consider yourself successful and strong, and in another, unimpressive and weak. Some days you think that your life is full of meaning, and on others, you wonder about your life's purpose. At times, you are energetic and happy, and hours later, you are lethargic and sad. At any given point, the self you think of as "you" is momentary and unstable. All of the labels and feelings that you attach to yourself, and often think of as "you," are not truly your essence.

It is undeniable that your essence would continue to exist even if your name were to disappear. Just as you might wear a hat and then take it off, or put on clothes and then take them off, you can actually change your identity as you choose.

To feel your true essence, try this simple "Erasing Meditation." It involves using your imagination to completely erase all of the information and images that you have acquired in the past in order to know who you truly are now. If possible, practice this meditation in a quiet, natural spot where you can fully concentrate without being interrupted.

First, write your name on a piece of paper and call out your name. As you do this, examine what words and feelings come into your mind. Write them on the paper. Do you have any strong emotions about any of the things you wrote down? Do any of the words or descriptions associated with your name ring particularly true or false for you?

Next, choose a tool in your mind's eye to use as a method of erasing all the things associated with your name. It might be a simple pencil eraser or the eraser tool in a computer graphic program.

What shall we erase first? Let's begin with our name. Close your eyes and imagine your name as you have written it on the paper. Call it out and then use your imaginary eraser to erase it. You no longer have a name.

What else would you like to change? Let's begin with what's visible: your body.

Close your eyes and begin to erase your body one part at a time. Start with your lower half. Erase your feet, ankles, calves, knees, and thighs. Is it going well? If not, continue to concentrate, and move slowly. If distracting thoughts come to mind while you are doing the erasing, delete those, too.

Now start erasing your arms, hands, wrists, and shoulders. Only your trunk and head are left. Wipe your entire trunk away. Now it's time to erase your head. Your head contains countless bits of information that form your ego. These include the skills and knowledge you have attained, ideas and memories you have formed, even needs and emotions that you have experienced. These are the things that you mistake for yourself, the "you" with whom you identify. While erasing your head, wipe them all away.

> Even with all the things erased, something still remains. It is the void that you originally are.

What is left? You have no body, no memories, and no emotions. You have no sadness and no joy. The thinking you itself is gone. You have nothing. Everything about your concept of you has disappeared and no longer exists.

Even with all these things erased, something still remains. The place from which your body disappeared is transparent because nothing is there, but that transparency reveals what is behind it. If you are in a natural place, then nature appears in the background; if you're in a room, then the transparency uncovers the room behind it. The transparency is empty space. It is the void that you originally are. You contain and reveal everything like the transparent void. In Korean, this void is called *Mu*, which means "nothingness" or "nonexistent."

The third realization to the Tao is knowing *Muah*. The *Mu* means "nonexistent" and the character *Ah* means "self." Taken literally, it means "the self does not exist." In this context, Mu does not indicate "absence," as in "something is not there." Like transparent space, it shows what is behind the very concepts of existence and non-existence. In other words, it is the state that exists before the concepts of "being" and "nonbeing." It is called "absolute nothingness." Absolute nothingness is not something that can be understood through our knowledge and reason, which seek to separate, define, and conceptualize things.

Many people fear the word Mu. To them, it seems as if their very being vanishes. They have no concept of absolute nothingness so, instantly, Mu makes them think of nonexistence.

If we want to express absolute nothingness metaphorically, we can use the example of a transparent screen. Suppose a transparent screen is in front of you. It cannot be touched or perceived as solid matter. It's just empty space. In short, you could say it's not there. It's not that nothing is there, though. This is because objects and phenomena exist with the screen as their background.

Let's say that you put a flower vase on the transparent screen. We would say that the flower vase exists. If we take a flower vase away from that spot, people would say that the flower vase was nonexistent. This is how the concepts of existence and nonexistence come into being. Relative concepts like being and nonbeing are created on the basis of absolute nothingness, which is like a transparent screen or empty space.

Absolute nothingness has never come into being, and so it does not disappear. "Appear" and "disappear" apply only to being. Everything that exists with absolute nothingness as its background appears and then disappears. Even time and space are relative things that exist on the background of absolute nothingness. That is why nothingness cannot be limited by the temporal concepts of beginning and end, and why it cannot be expressed by the spatial concepts of big and small. If we insist on describing it in temporal terms, then we would say that, although it is the beginning, it is the beginning with no beginning, and although it is the end, it is the end with no end. If we describe it in spatial terms, then we must say that nothingness is bigger than the biggest thing and smaller than the smallest thing.

Nothingness is within everything we see, hear, and know. We are always seeing, feeling, and breathing nothingness. It is not something far off or hidden. We merely have trouble perceiving it because it is so close and so obvious.

Absolute nothingness is the world of life energy that comprises everything in the cosmos. Energy forms matter when it comes together, and we perceive that as "being." Conversely, when the energy of some matter disperses, we no longer see that matter, and we perceive it as not existing. Being and nonbeing are phenomena created by energy, and their essence is life energy, which is the ground of being. Everything in the world appears and disappears on the backdrop of this life energy.

> Absolute nothingness is the world of life energy that comprises everything in the cosmos.

Absolute nothingness is like empty space. Although it appears completely empty, space surrounds and embraces everything existing in the world. Empty space also fills everything in the world. For example, let's say that we have a ripe, red apple. To your eyes, the apple appears to be solid and three dimensional, consisting of firm flesh and sweet juice. But if we magnify a slice of the apple thousands of times, it appears to be full of holes, like a sponge. Under this intense scrutiny, the apple is merely a lump of vibrating energy.

The structure of the atom illustrates this. An atom is made up of neutrons, protons, and electrons. Between these particles within the atom there exists empty space. If a hydrogen atom were the size of a soccer stadium, then its nucleus, which contains the protons and electrons, would be the size of a ping-pong ball, and its electron, which orbits the nucleus, would be ten kilometers away from the nucleus. Within the atom, nothing but empty space exists between the nucleus and the electrons. But it's not that nothing exists in that space; incredible, immeasurable energy vibrates there dynamically. In other words, it is a state of complete empty fullness.

Energy doesn't only fill space inside matter. It also fills the space that exists outside matter, the empty space that is usually invisible to the naked eye, but is sometimes perceived as visible by those who are more sensitive to energy. For example, auras are actually made up of energy that circulates in the empty pace outside of matter. Once you develop a sense for seeing this energy, when you view empty space objectively, you can see momentary flashes of light, like rapidly dancing vortexes filling the void.

Thus, the void, or energy, is both inside and outside all matter in existence. It is present everywhere. The void seems to be completely empty, but it is actually filled by the life energy of the cosmos—the infinite, self-existent great life force of the cosmos, Mu (nothingness). This is your true essence. When you escape from the finite self you have understood to be you, you come to experience your third realization concerning the Tao; Muah—awakening to the selfless nature of existence—and you become one with the infinite life energy of the cosmos, which is your essence, in a state in which your ego does not exist.

Muah and a Life of Creation

Why do we seek to awaken to the selfless nature of who we are, and why should we? Life, it has been said, is characterized by suffering and impermanence. It is unfortunate enough to have been born into this world, but even more unfortunate is a life lived without knowing its meaning and purpose, not to mention a life lived without knowing where we go when we die. Once we directly face the truth that life is continuous suffering and change, we feel a deep sense of emptiness. Those feelings of emptiness are a sign that the thick shell surrounding your soul is starting to break.

Life is suffering and all things change. What have we come here for? Can't we escape from suffering and impermanence? The realization that allows us to escape from suffering and impermanence is Muah, for all anguish and delusion arise out of the ego. Muah is a state of freedom from the attachments of the ego.

It's easy, and common, for people to think that attaining Muah means that the self disappears. That's not so, however. Muah is an expansion from the small self into a greater Self. Everyone has probably felt a sense of constricted frustration, as if they were trapped within some limit or mold, and wanted to escape from it. The way to escape from the limits of that self is to attain Muah, in other words, to connect with the infinite, vast life energy of the cosmos. This is a state like the void, which is full although it seems completely empty, one in which the "self" does not actually exist. It's feeling that, even amid nonexistence, the infinite, self-existent life force of the cosmos is the substance of who you are.

> The way to escape from the limits of the small self is to attain Muah, connecting with the infinite life energy.

We can engage in true creation by awakening to Muah. Our thinking cannot help but be limited and rigid when we are trapped within the self we know, in the self we have experienced. Our minds open and become more peaceful, and we feel an unknowable joy and vitality well up within us when we are connected with the life energy of the universe. Like the flow of the energy that vibrates and moves without ever resting, our thoughts escape their previous limits and molds to become more flexible, creative, and freer.

You may have had times when you struggled because ideas wouldn't come to mind when you were planning some work or project. At such times, take a walk for a while, and then, unexpectedly, good ideas will come to mind. As you walk, you will let go of your tangled thoughts and find new inspiration because you will be refreshed with the fresh energy of nature.

Connecting with the energy of nature is the easiest way to connect with the life energy of the cosmos and attain Muah. Energy training methods like meditation, breathing, and kigong, which involve opening the energy points, channels, and chakras in your body to accept and circulate the life energy of the cosmos, are both profound and extremely effective.

An important tip for receiving cosmic energy is this: open your mind and empty yourself of thoughts, ideas, and emotions. In accordance with the principle of Shim Ki Hyul Jung—which means that, where the mind goes, energy follows—if you close your mind and fill it with your own thoughts, ideas, and emotions, there is no way pure cosmic energy will enter it. If you are to receive it, you must open and empty your mind. Something new will start to fill the place that has been emptied. I'm stressing that to attain a state of Muah, you must empty your ego—what you think of as yourself.

Vast, infinite life energy enters and fills that place emptied of your ego. It is being upgraded from your small self to your great Self.

Receiving cosmic energy can be compared to rice farmers irrigating a rice paddy. Rice grows in paddies filled with water. That's why farmers fight during droughts; they even battle with the owners of neighboring fields, struggling with each other to bring into their paddies the water that fills surrounding ditches. But the farmers of villages that have a massive reservoir above their paddies have nothing over which to fight each other. They can always get along because they irrigate their crops using plentiful water from the reservoir.

Our connecting with the life energy of the cosmos is like this. People try hard to create something and lead their lives through their own thoughts and energy, trapped within the narrow confines of their own egos. It's like a farmer who irrigates his crops with the trickle of water flowing in the little ditches around his fields. Others go so far as to close the doors of their minds, living in resentment of an unfair world. Closing your mind is the same as blocking the channel through which energy can enter.

> To attain a state of Muah, you must empty your ego, what you think of as yourself.

We have an incredibly vast reservoir that never runs dry. It is the infinite, eternal life energy of the universe. We don't need to battle over that source, for it is infinite and accessible to anyone. All you have to do is access and download energy from that source in a state in which your body and mind are open and emptied of tangled thoughts and emotions.

Life pours out of the bodies and minds of people connected with cosmic energy. Their eyes sparkle; their faces have bright, kindly smiles; their hearts are filled with love and passion. Creative inspiration and ideas well up within them because of their flexible, free thinking. More than anything else, they seek to use as much of the life energy and vast cosmic energy that have been given to them as possible to do meaningful, valuable work that contributes to the life energy field of the whole. They know that other people and themselves—their environment and themselves—are not separate, but are connected within a single, massive energy field. This is expressed as love for all, as a love that comes from Muah or selflessness, from a state emptied of self.

We finally gain the wisdom to escape from the suffering and impermanence of life when we know the selfless nature of existence. Although the original landscape of our lives is painted with suffering and impermanence, when we awaken to our own selfless natures and become one with the life energy of the cosmos, this changes into a landscape of blessing. When we attract to ourselves the energy of life, we can truly create our own lives.

Enlightenment and spiritual realization are not visible to the eyes. They are expressed and demonstrated through the moment-by-moment choices in our lives. We can gradually learn how to become the true creators of our lives by choosing in every moment with an awareness of selflessness. That is the life of the Tao.

CHAPTER TEN

The Illusion of Death

ONE OF THE MOST SIGNIFICANT QUESTIONS people ask about the nature of life is "What happens after I die?" Everyone already knows what the experience of birth brings, but no one is truly certain about the nature of the afterlife. Although no one knows exactly when or how death will occur, we all inevitably meet with this fate. Death is simply a fact of life beyond the powers of human beings to control. While many of us in our youth thought that our lives would last forever, we all must eventually accept that life in its physical form is a finite experience.

The longest-living person whose dates of birth and death were verified in the Guinness World Records lived to be 122. According to the UN World Health Organization's World Health Statistics 2014, a girl born in 2012 can expect to live about seventy-three years and a boy about sixty-eight years. Life expectancy in the United States for females is eighty-one years, and for males it's seventy-six years. If you are destined to live an average lifespan, how many years do you have left?

Even if you think that you have as many as forty years left according to the average life span statistics, you can never be sure when your time to meet death will actually come.

Death is an uncomfortable topic for most people. But because we will all experience it someday, it behooves us to contemplate the issue from time to time. While I do not advocate that you dwell on the issue, it is good to consider whether, when you are on your deathbed, you will be able to look back and feel proud of the way you have lived your life. Coming to terms with the inevitable cycle of life and death helps us to live in a good way.

About fifteen years ago I went to Nepal with a friend. While I was there, I saw a fascinating item in a souvenir shop—a bowl decorated with silver and beads of different colors. When I asked the shopkeeper about it, she said it was a dish for holding food. And when I asked what it was made of, she replied that it was made from a human skull.

Can you imagine eating food, a symbol of life, from a container made from a human skull? To most people, the human skull signifies death. The bowl reflects the wisdom of the Nepalese people, who acknowledge that death is always a part of life. The bowl reminds its user to consider that each moment of life is precious. With this in mind, wouldn't you work hard to make something significant of your life?

Life and Death Are an Illusion

Many people think that life begins the moment we are born and ends at the moment of death. We think that our lives have a clear starting and ending point, like a precisely measured piece of wood. This seems logical because we can only perceive and experience the world from the standpoint of our physical form. It seems as though our perception of physical reality is all there is and that everything ends with death.

> Coming to terms with the inevitable cycle of life and death helps us to live in a good way.

When do you think your physical life began? Many people think that life begins at the moment of birth. But didn't your life exist before then? Didn't you spend nine months as a fetus in your mother's womb? Should you then view your life as beginning in the instant your parents' egg and sperm met each other? Did that sperm and egg suddenly appear out of nowhere? Of course not. The sperm that helped give rise to your life was a part of your father's life, arising out of his body's cells. Likewise, the egg that divided over and over again to form your body was at first part of your mother's body. So all of life connects endlessly to the cycle of life, and so it continues back through the generations, no matter how far back we go, until we reach the source of life itself.

But what marked the beginning of your spiritual life, your soul's encounter with your body? There are many different views about when the soul connects with the body. Some believe that it happens when the sperm first fertilizes the egg; others believe it occurs once the fetus takes on human form; and still others say the soul enters the body when we take our first breath outside the womb. Although no one can confirm any of these beliefs with certainty, most of us agree that we all have some kind of innate spirit, a "soul," that animates our human form.

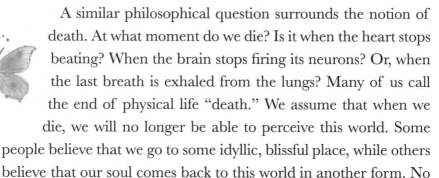

A similar philosophical question surrounds the notion of death. At what moment do we die? Is it when the heart stops beating? When the brain stops firing its neurons? Or, when the last breath is exhaled from the lungs? Many of us call the end of physical life "death." We assume that when we die, we will no longer be able to perceive this world. Some people believe that we go to some idyllic, blissful place, while others believe that our soul comes back to this world in another form. No one really knows. Perhaps after the physical body dies, our consciousness remains and can perceive the invisible world, as well as the physical one.

In spite of such beliefs in the afterlife, many people fear death. We associate it with a cold, sad, dark and dreary place. Such feelings come from the illusions of our sensory phenomena. We imagine a stiff body being closed up in a dark coffin and lowered into the cold ground. This perception is normal for people who are raised in a culture where the belief systems are centered on the physical form. In cultures that view the body as simply a shell that houses the soul, however, death is not such a scary place.

Many of our images concerning death come from religious dogma. They depict what happens to a person after death in one of two ways: 1) a person's soul falls into a hot underworld of fire and brimstone called Hell where they are doomed to spend eternity as punishment for their sins, or 2) their soul ascends a white staircase and enters a place called Heaven, a transcendental realm where they meet an omniscient being and reside forever without suffering. The fear

> The energy that animates life does not vanish, but merely changes and circulates in a different form.

of eternal punishment is not the real reason people fear it, however. The real problem is that it is an unknown that exists beyond this realm. This uncomfortable state of unknowing gives rise to all sorts of elaborate cultural customs, dogmatic religious beliefs, and fearful prejudices.

No one can definitively tell you what really happens after death. There are those who say that they have been on the verge of death, and even those who claim to have glimpsed the afterlife in a near-death experience. But even these people have not experienced the finite state that we call death. They almost died, but they did not permanently pass into the afterlife, which is the true meaning of death.

In the perspective of energy, the energy that animates life does not vanish with death. It merely changes and circulates in a different form. For example, imagine that your family buries your body beneath a rose bush. In time, your body decays and becomes part of the soil that covers the roots of the rose bush. When it rains, the rose bush soaks up nutrients from the soil and, in essence, your body becomes part of the plant. If part of the soil washes into a nearby stream, your body becomes part of the ecosystem that nourishes other plants and animals. The water that was in your body becomes part of the water vapor that evaporates into the clouds and thus part of your body also becomes rain. The elements that make up the human body continue to move and circulate long after death, becoming an energy source for the natural world.

During your life, many energy sources from the natural world (air, water, plants, and animals) supported and sustained your life. The fruit, vegetables, grain, and meat you ate became part of your body. The air you breathed and the water you drank became a part of you. In the same way, someday you will also become an energy source for other life forms. We are part of a never-ending cycle and circle of life.

Similarly, the human soul transforms itself and is never-ending. In Korea, the expression Hon Bi Baek San means that the soul flies and the body scatters. Upon death, the human soul is separated from the body, and the physical form known as our body disperses, becoming a natural source of energy. What, then, happens to the human soul separated from the body? The soul follows natural laws of energy. If you take a glass cup containing muddy water and let it sit, the heavier, cloudy particles will sink to the bottom, while the clear, lighter particles will rise upward. In the same way, our souls go to environments appropriate to their energy states.

People commonly think that dying and "going to heaven" is equivalent to obtaining eternal life. From the Tao perspective, life energy exists eternally, whether it is light or dense energy. The only difference between the two is the dimensions in which they exist. They are different depending on whether they exist as bright, clear energy or as dark, cloudy energy.

Human life energy is not finite. It cannot be separated from the Universal life force that makes up the cosmos. This is true for all life forms, whether plants, animals, humans, or microorganisms. Life energy is like the electricity that powers a light bulb. When life energy enters a physical body, that is the start of a life; when it separates from the physical body, that is death. Life and death are like a light bulb being turned on and off. Electricity itself does not cease to exist simply because the lights in your house go out. Electrical energy still exists even when the lights go out. Thus, it's a mistake to believe that life and death are somehow separate from the life energy of the cosmos. Our perception of life and death is nothing but an illusion.

> There is no life and death separate from the infinite life energy of the cosmos.

Life energy flows infinitely. What we commonly refer to as "life and death" are actually just boundaries between two states. In one state, energy is coming together; this is called life. In the other, it is dispersing; this is called death. When the energy of the spirit encounters the physical body, it becomes a distinct, visible life. When the energy of the spirit separates from the body and disperses, it becomes invisible and is marked by the physical phenomenon we call death. That energy, however, continues to exist.

In reality, we don't die, but merely change. Energy reveals and hides itself repeatedly as it flows along. The flame of life flickers on and off, again and again. How could the flame going out for a brief time signify extinction? There is no life and death separate from the infinite life energy of the cosmos. The phenomena of life energy merely change and cycle in accordance with the law of infinite energy.

On Past Lives and Reincarnation

Do you believe in past lives and reincarnation? Similar to the concept of death, many people are curious about this subject. And, just like all the other theories about life after death, there is no way to scientifically prove whether it actually exists. Still, many people believe in these concepts and some even claim they have glimpsed their own or someone else's past or future life.

Personally, I believe in past lives and reincarnation. But I am not here to convince you or force my beliefs on you. Only this matters: your perspective on past lives and reincarnation should contribute to your personal and spiritual growth.

A friend of mine who suffered from lung cancer is a case in point. One day, on a trip to a gallery in New Mexico, he asked a Native American healer for a past life reading. Although he made no mention of his illness, the healer told him this: "You died from a serious disease in your chest 300 years ago. You could suffer from the same serious disease in your chest area in this life, too, if your soul recalls a memory of your past life. Be kind and generous to those around you, and do a lot of praying and meditation. Then you will gradually be purified of your past life memories and attachments."

Upon hearing the healer's words, my friend felt a sense of liberation, as if the weight of decades had been lifted from his shoulders. A few months later, his lung cancer had completely vanished. There is no way to know whether the healer's words were true, but the information about a past life changed my friend's attitude and cured him of his disease.

In contrast with my friend's case, if your own story of a past life interferes with your focusing on your present life, then you don't need to believe it. Having excessive curiosity and fantasies about past lives could be a stumbling block that keeps you from focusing on the present. If believing in past lives contributes to your life and spiritual growth, then believe in them; if it doesn't, then don't. What's important is making choices that fully benefit your present life.

Even though this is not the general definition of a past life, our parents, grandparents, and all our ancestors could also be considered part of our past lives. Similarly, you could say that your children, or the experiences and footprints you leave behind, are your reincarnations. Just as those who lived before left us the world we have today, we will leave behind the world of tomorrow for the generations that follow. When we consider it this way, our lives are linked with those of others thousands of years in the past and thousands of years in the future. Thus, rather than being lost in thoughts about past lives and reincarnation, we must focus on creating a better future by living honest, sincere, and responsible lives now.

> Your perspective on past lives and reincarnation should contribute to your personal and spiritual growth.

A famous Korean Taekwondo master who was active in America came to see me in Korea. We talked a lot and became close. He wanted to visit Mt. Moak, where I had engaged in twenty-one days of aesthetic practice, so we headed for the mountain together. On the way, I said to him, "When we get to Mt. Moak, you'll be able to see a tomato becoming a person when the moon is full." Although he was doubtful, he wore an expression full of expectation and curiosity.

On our way up the mountain, we saw children eating tomatos. That's when he traded with the kids: candies for tomatos for quenching his thirst. The full moon rose over Mt. Moak that night. Sitting on a rock and looking up at the full moon as he meditated, the martial artist seemed to be waiting for something mysterious to happen. It was almost midnight, but I had said nothing. As if unable to bear it any longer, he asked, "When will I see a tomato becoming a person?"

Barely able to control my laughter, I said, "I'm watching it right now. You ate a tomato a while ago. Hasn't that tomato now become you?" He let out a great laugh, finally getting my point.

Our life energy doesn't cease to exist, but merely changes form and cycles continuously in accordance with the law of energy. In this sense, we reincarnate endlessly as either visible or invisible energy.

On Karma

What is Karma and how does it develop? Karma, as spoken of in Buddhism and Hinduism, relates to the universal law of cause and effect. This means that for every action, there is an equal and opposite reaction. Karma is the resulting effect of our words, deeds, actions, and experiences. If we practice good deeds, allowing compassion and altruism to guide our actions in life, we are said to be creating good Karma. However, if our life is driven by the ego, and we use our brains to exploit others, do harm, and cause destruction to the world around us, we are creating bad Karma.

In theological terms, Karma is the cosmic principle by which a person is rewarded or punished in one incarnation according to that person's deeds in a previous incarnation. Karma can also refer to the good or bad emanations that you might feel being generated by someone or something. In Buddhist philosophy, while some souls may reincarnate back into this physical world, others become so enlightened that they may stay in higher realms. The lesson of Karma is to clear Karma in this life so that if you do come back, you come back in the best possible way, or if you no longer have Karma to clear, your soul goes on to another, higher realm.

Even if you do not believe in past lives or Karma, you can likely accept that the temperaments of your ancestors have been passed down to you through genetics and through patterns of family behavior. To put it simply, I think that karma is "temperament." The Korean word for temperament is *Kijil*, meaning "nature or quality of energy." Kijil refers to one's character or personality.

When you were young, did your mother ever say to you, "You are just like your father. I have never seen anyone as stubborn as the two of you."? Or perhaps another relative observed, "You are so talented and artistic, just like your mother." We inherit aspects of our temperament from our parents and grandparents, both from their genes and from the belief systems they instill in us. By early childhood, we have already acquired most of the habitual thought patterns and beliefs that will affect us throughout the rest of our adult lives—that is, unless we make a conscious effort to change them.

> In order to change your temperament, Karma, you must purify and improve the quality of your energy.

In order to change your temperament, you must purify and improve the quality of your energy, making it lighter and clearer. This is difficult to do when we are driven by the belief systems, attachments, and desires of our ego. For example, imagine a person who grew up experiencing a great deal of hardship because his or her family was extremely poor. Often, such people will have a tremendous attachment to money. This attachment dictates all their actions involving money and, depending on their choices, can cause good or bad Karma. Unless the attachment is released, this temperament can be passed down to their descendants as genetic or epigenetic inheritances.

Karma can have many layers. As we work on abandoning our attachments and letting go of our egos, we peel off one layer only to reveal another. We also create new Karma every day with our actions. Taking off a layer of Karma is not as easy as taking off clothes. Most people equate their personal identity with their Karma, since it strongly adheres to them in the form of their ideas, emotions, and habits. Thus, things like selfishness, pride, and negative emotions arise to resist others who activate their Karma.

In order to release ourselves from our Karma, we must first awaken to the fact that our ideas, emotions, and habits—which give rise to Karmic reactions—are not the essence of who we are. And this awakening must not remain only in our heads. It must sink down into our hearts and change our temperament and our energy. Then, it must descend all the way to the lower Dahnjon to change our habits and behaviors. To accomplish this, we engage in the three kinds of study: the Study of Principle, to learn with our intellect; the Study of Practice, to change our energy; and the Study of Living, to change our habits and behaviors.

Unburdening yourself of Karma is not an abstract concept. It's simply a matter of changing bad habits one at a time. Unhealthy habits are nothing more than obstacles standing in the way of your soul's growth. As we live our lives, we continually build up layers of Karma unless we correct our habits. The habits you've built since coming into this world can be called the report card of your soul for this life. If you take action to change them one by one, each cell in your body will also change. This practice of concretely changing your life as you develop your soul's power in the course of conquering habits is the Study of Living.

A good Study of Living for clearing past Karma is to live a life of sharing. By sharing your compassion from a loving, unconditional heart, you create good Karma. There are generally three things we can share with others. First, you can teach the principles of enlightenment. Second you can heal the minds and bodies of those who are suffering by alleviating their pain. Third, you can provide material aid, the way you do when you donate food or money to people in need.

> A good Study of Living for clearing past Karma is to live a life of sharing.

We can commit to doing at least one of these three things. If there are principles that you have studied and learned so far, then share them. If you can heal the bodies and minds of others with love, then share the energy of love. If you have enough material wealth to share with others, then do so. No matter how long you sit around meditating with your legs crossed, you cannot escape your Karma without such action. That's why I say, "Sharing is real practice."

But doing good deeds with some expectation of reward can create bad Karma. If you seek recognition by boasting to others of the good deeds you have done, if you resent the person and say, "I did this for you, why don't you do something for me in return?" or if you think, "I'll go to heaven if I do these good deeds," that is, if you are greedy for reward in whatever form, it turns into bad Karma.

If you do a bad deed, you can repent once you know what you have done wrong. If you do a good deed out of a desire for reward, however, you believe you have done well, and, far from repenting, you actually become proud and boastful. That is why Jesus taught: "Do not let your left hand know what your right is doing." Genuine sharing arises on its own out of an unconditionally true heart, not out of a desire for reward.

To share with a genuine heart, it must be done from the perspective of Muah consciousness. Muah consciousness is a state free of worldly desires. It facilitated tremendous flow of life energy beyond duality, where there is no you or me, no good or bad, and no arguing about who is right. In the truest reality, you and I are not two separate beings, but rather one life energy, so there is no need to do good deeds out of a sense of obligation. Rather, compassion and love arise spontaneously, as if you were simply helping yourself. When we love others and build personal relationships from a place of this Muah consciousness, before we know it, we form good habits, our temperament is purified, and our Karma is cleared a little bit at a time.

On the End and Eternal Life

There is no need to bring up the apocalyptic dogma of religions and prophets; environmental scientists and international organizations, such as the United Nations and environmental non-profits, warn us that if we continue on our current course, a great disaster will befall the planet. Just as people are bound to become ill when they are tired and worn out, the results of a deteriorating global environment will inevitably express itself in one form or another.

It won't do any good to pray to a god, asking him to keep the end from coming, because the situation was not created intentionally by god to punish humanity. No such god, as human beings think of him with intentions and emotions, exists. If the end of the world does come, it will be the result of human impact, such as environmental pollution, nuclear war, and infectious disease. Energy within the earth or the cosmos at large will shift as an automatic result of us failing to act in accordance with nature's balance.

How will you feel if the planet is hit by a great disaster? In the movie *2012*, when Earth comes to an end, the wealthy elite of the world pay a huge price to board a modern version of Noah's Ark, the only perceived means of survival. Although the people save their own lives in a moment of crisis, that is not eternal life. Ultimately, they are also human beings who cannot escape the destiny of death.

Many people worry about their physical death, but they are not as concerned about dying before realizing the essence of their souls. But this in fact should be their greatest concern. If they fail to realize the essence of their souls, though they live, they don't live; and though they die, they don't die. No person ever truly lives until they realize the essence of the soul. If a person fails to realize the essence of his or her soul, death will not set the soul free.

> Though those who have awakened to the essence of their souls die physically, they do not truly die.

Conversely, though those who have awakened to the essence of their souls die physically at the end of their lives, they do not truly die. If a person already has Muah consciousness, which transcends physical life and death, the death of the body has little meaning. She knows her soul, her life energy, and becomes one with the eternal life energy of the universe. Many people worry about death and are anxious about the end of humanity because they don't understand that the soul is immortal with the eternal life energy.

Even if the end comes, the universal energy of the cosmos will still exist. While the three-dimensional reality of time and space appears to be finite, the absolute consciousness of Muah is infinite. The essence of the soul is Muah, which has no beginning and no end. If you knew the world of Muah, you wouldn't worry about your mortality.

Some people think eternal life is dependent upon believing some particular dogma. According to them, anyone who fails to accept those beliefs, whatever they may be, is doomed to die. These people don't understand the principles of nature. In reality, you don't need to believe in something. Just awaken to the essence of who you are, which exists without beginning and without end. Why would you tie yourself down with thoughts of life and death when you know that there is no such thing, and that the great life energy of the universe is the essence of who you are?

All souls are eternal. This is a natural law of energy. The soul's energy, whether good or bad, is never destroyed. It can, however, be transmuted. The form that it takes is your choice. Will your eternal energy be bright and clear, or dark and dense? In accordance with the laws of energy, light, bright souls go where the nature of their energy takes them, while heavy, dark souls go to a place appropriate for the nature of their energy. Clear water rises upward, while turbid, muddy water sinks downward; light water vapor rises up, while heavy rain water falls down. The principle is the same. The law of energy is a precise transaction, and, so, there is no bargaining.

The brightness of our consciousness while in our physical life form determines the dimension of our afterlife. This is why it's important to lead a life of compassion and goodness and to work toward the growth and completion of your soul. We do this, as mentioned previously, through the three Studies of Principle,

Practice, and Living.

Humans are most joyful when they are living from the heart, listening to their soul's guidance, and contributing meaningfully to society. To have a dream or vision for one's life is essential to the growth of the soul. For those who have no hopes or dreams, repeating the same life continuously is nothing but drudgery.

No one knows when they will die. This is why it's important to be truly present in each moment and to live each day to its fullest.

> The brightness of our consciousness while in our physical life form determines the dimension of our afterlife.

Parents should teach their children wisdom concerning death If parents are fearful of death, the reality of death will be distressful for their children, too. On their deathbeds, they should be able to say to their kids, "I've lived a meaningful life, so death does not scare me. Please do not cry when I die. I'm happy to be casting off my body. Why shed tears? Don't be sad, just play some beautiful music."

If they are able to say this, as they quietly control their breathing and leave their body, what a wonderful and peaceful death that will be.

The Dream of Chunhwa

What kind of death do you want to experience? This is the same as asking, "What kind of life do you want to live?" How you live your life determines the quality of your death. In the same way that people live life on different levels, our deaths occur on many different levels, too. In Korea, there are various expressions that reveal the level of a person's death. The level of death serves as a basis for evaluating the person's life, not for evaluating the death itself.

First, the expression Dwejida is similar to the slang term croaked in English. It means that you became what you should have become, or went where you should have gone, but in a negative sense. It's used to describe the death of a person who has not lived a good life—someone who has committed significant crimes, or who has seriously hurt those around him. People actually welcome this person's death and feel a sense of relief from his passing. It is an expression referring to those who have lived their lives at a lower level, one not worthy of human beings.

The second expression is Jukda, which is equivalent to the simple English verb "to die." It is used to describe people who have lived an ordinary life, without really helping or hurting those around them.

Third is the expression Dolahgashida, which is equivalent to the English phrase to pass away. It is used to express mourning for the death of a parent or elder. This person has achieved some degree of completion in terms of their personal character and has lived as a decent human being. "To die" and "pass away" are expressions that describe the death of a person whose consciousness has remained at the level of Hyo.

The fourth expression is Seogeo, which is used to refer to the death of a person who has contributed significantly to society or a nation, and who has met death after living life with his a consciousness at the level of Choong.

Fifth is the expression, Chunhwa, which refers to a death of the highest level. The word Chun means "heaven" and Hwa means "become." Together, Chunhwa means "one who has become heaven," which could be translated as "Heavenly Transformation." Here heaven can be expressed as the Tao, the Divine, the Source, full consciousness, etc. Chunhwa signifies the death of a person who has genuinely realized the principles of the cosmos and the purpose of life, and who has reached a level of Tao consciousness for the completion of his or her soul.

What kind of death do you desire? There is no way to know whether being born into this world was your conscious choice in another dimension or just a principle of nature. One thing is certain, however: only you can choose how you will meet death. You alone can choose what level of death you experience. No one can judge your choice on this matter, and no one can help you determine your type of death. It will be determined solely by the way you live your life and the level of consciousness that you attain.

> Death is not an ending, but a return to the fundamental life source.

Chunhwa describes an awakening to your own divinity, after which you will return to the cosmic Source from which you came. To achieve this, you must awaken to the universal life force, the cosmic energy from which you sprang. Those who experience Chunhwa know that life and death are an illusion. To them, death is not an ending, but a return to the fundamental life source.

An ancient Korean scripture, the Chun Bu Kyung, tells of the meaning and process of Chunhwa through a text of eighty-one characters. The first verse of Chun Bu Kyung is "Il Shi Mu Shi Il," which means "Everything begins in one, but that one has no beginning," and the last verse of it is "Il Jong Mu Jong Il," which means "Everything ends in one, but that one is without ending."

The heart of the Chun Bu Kyung is suggested by the word Il, which means "One, but one that contains all." The one is where all creation begins and where all creation ends, but it is the great life energy of the cosmos, eternally self-existent, without beginning and without end.

The process of how all creation arises out of the one and returns to the one is described in the Chun Bu Kyung. Toward the end of the text, we find the expression, Myo Yeon Man Wang Man Rae, Yong Byun Bu Dong Bon. This means, "All things mysteriously come and go within the order of the universe, and, although their purposes change, their original nature does not change." All creation continuously moves and recycles, changing form and function. Still, the original nature of this life does not change; it is endless.

So, what is this changeless original nature? Let's look at the next verse in the Chun Bu Kyung: Bon Shim Bon Tae Yang. It means, "The original mind is bright like the sun." Because the original mind, or original nature, is bright like the sun, human consciousness also becomes brighter once it realizes that the original mind is within itself. What happens when we have a consciousness that is as bright as the sun?

Chun Bu Kyung describes In Joong Chun Ji Il, which means, "Heaven and earth exist within humanity, and the three are one." Those whose consciousness is as bright as the sun know that both heaven and earth are found within humanity.

The Chun Bu Kyung ends with Il Jong Mu Jong Il, which means, "Everything ends in one, but that one is without ending."

All things begin in the one—the Source—and pass through a process of creation and evolution, returning again to the one. That one, however, does not end; it exists eternally. Going back to the place we came from, to the state of perfect unity, is "Chunhwa."

Despite the fact that humans are beings full of selfish desires and emotions, have a body that is doomed to die in futility one day, suffer in endless pain, and are lonely amid impermanence, they have a great dream. It is the "Dream of Chunhwa." It is the dream of escaping from the finiteness of our existence to complete our souls and to return to the place from where we came. Chunhwa is the goal of human life, and it should be what we aspire to in death.

The metamorphosis of a caterpillar becoming a butterfly reflects the process of Chunhwa. At first, the caterpillar is an egg. When it breaks out of its egg, the caterpillar diligently eats leaves in order to survive. What's amazing, though, is that after it has finished growing and has reached its full length and weight, the caterpillar pulls a thread from its own body and starts creating a cocoon or molts into a shiny chrysalis. Then it waits a long time, transforming rapidly as it endures without eating. One day, it squeezes itself out of its cocoon or chrysalis and emerges as a beautiful butterfly. Then it spreads its brilliant wings and soars into the sky.

> Going back to the place we came from, to the state of perfect unity, is "Chunhwa."

Amazingly, the caterpillar that once crawled around on the ground and wasn't much to look at changes into a beautiful butterfly that can fly freely to its heart's content! We can't help but be surprised by the mystery of life, for hidden within that caterpillar are factors enabling it to become a butterfly. Just as a caterpillar changes into a beautiful butterfly, so can humans escape from the finiteness of their existence. They can experience Chunhwa to become one with the infinite life energy of the universe.

Remember, however, that caterpillars cannot suddenly become butterflies in a day. Just as a caterpillar spends a significant amount of time spinning its cocoon and preparing to be reborn into a more beautiful existence, so too must we devote time and diligence to the growth of our souls.

The three studies that you do for the growth of your soul facilitate just such a process. Pulling a thread of life energy from your body, you fill your lower Dahnjon with Jung energy, mature the Ki energy of your middle Dahnjon, and brighten the Shin energy of your upper Dahnjon. You have within you humanity's original dream to become one with the essence of the Cosmos and to return to the cosmic Source. This is the dream of Chunhwa.

The Blessing of Death

Death is a powerful and frightening concept in a finite world. But in the infinite world of energy, our current life is nothing more than a journey. What is certain is that the time period for this journey is set. Although we don't know exactly when, one day our souls will have to leave our bodies without any regrets. We can take nothing with us when we go. We have to leave behind all the money, prestige, and

power we have gained in this world. We cannot take with us even a strand of hair from the bodies we have always fed, clothed, put to sleep, and cared for.

In the face of death, even endless human desire is completely humbled. Desire is merely a fleeting fantasy for maintaining life. You may live your life in a fantasy and then regret it before death, but by that time it will be too late. If we were to fully admit that we cannot cheat death, we would live our lives more consciously and passionately. We would savor every moment as precious.

Death helps us put perspective on life. If it were not for death and the finite nature that it adds to our physical existence, we might not thirst to know something infinite, something able to overcome their finiteness. We might not seek so earnestly to experience enlightenment and to truly know the meaning of Tao, the law of eternal life energy.

We develop a thirst for the Tao because we do not know what is beyond this physical plane. It is our way of seeking an eternal existence during a short mortal life. Death can be considered a blessing to life because it is the nature of the unknown, the afterlife, that encourages us to become better people, to live a life of humility and compassion. Death lies at the bottom of our thirst for enlightenment, our thirst for completion of the soul. When we awaken to the principles of life, we begin to view death as just another extension of life. So death is a blessing for enlightenment, and for the completion of the soul.

> Death is a blessing for enlightenment, and for the completion of the soul.

The river of life flows endlessly. No one knows when the waters began to flow or when they will cease. Just as the waters of a river naturally flow toward the ocean, so will our lives meet a larger end. For those who know the Way of Chunhwa, this larger end does not represent death but rather an "Ocean of Life." It is a beautiful ocean of life filled with infinite and unbridled energy. Life is a journey to encounter the Ocean of Life. When we awaken to the principles of life, we realize that death is another extension of life. Death is not the end, but a new beginning. It is the rebirth of the completed soul, returning to the home from which it originally came.

We will all meet the beautiful Ocean of Life someday. We are given the gift of life and a free will to design it as we wish, to shape it into anything we want it to be. By creating the nature of our lives, we can choose the level of death that we experience. Because of this, we are not meaningless beings. We are co-creators of our world, co-creators of our universe. But unless we develop meaning and purpose in our lives, we will be unable to fully utilize and experience the creative potential we have been granted.

Imagine that you will be asked the following question at the moment of your death: "Did you live a good life?" What will be your answer? What values will you base your answer on? It is diffi-cult to answer this question without a standard of measure. Examine your life and ask yourself what standard you will use to measure the meaning of your life. Will your assessment be based on material, physical accomplishments, or will it be based upon the growth of your soul? Finding your own answer is the quickest way to create a joyful journey out of life instead of spending it wandering aimlessly.

Just as there are sea routes for boats and air routes for planes, there are also roads that people must travel as people. What is the road that a person should travel? That road is connected with the purpose of life and our existential value. What will be your path? Will you leave something of value behind, or will you have simply let the value of this life pass you by?

Eternity in a Moment

When considering the phenomenon of death, it is helpful to understand that the concepts of both life and death are merely illusions. We are nothing but endless cosmic energy manifesting for a brief time in physical form. Thus, living fully requires being "in the moment," present to the here and now, without being attached to life or worried about death. Those who are unable to be present in life experience much anger, torment, and sadness over things about which they have no control. We can't change our past or control our future with any kind of certainty or permanence. We must therefore take advantage of this physical experience while we can.

Even the word present is very vague. What does it really mean? The boundary of the present, when it begins and when it ends, is unclear. Mixed within what we call the present are the final threads of the past and the starting point of the future. The only way to experience the present is to quiet our minds so that we can experience the void between the breath. It is that place between thinking and not-thinking. It is no-thing.

Past and future are merely illusions. No matter how beautiful or painful the past may have been, it is already past. No matter how wonderful or awful we anticipate the future to be, it has not yet come. Neither exists in the present moment.

> The way to experience the present is to quiet our minds so that we can experience the void between the breath.

Many people have lost their ability to be in the here and now. For them, information about past and future has robbed them of the present moment. They have lost the ability to perceive their own mind objectively. To them, the "mind" is synonymous with "me." To shift this perspective, you must develop the ability to observe your thoughts and come back to the present moment. When your mind is running rampant with delusion, stop and breathe deeply and observe, "This mind is mine, but it is not me." Then ask yourself, "What am I thinking? What am I doing now? Am I in the present moment?"

How are you living today? Can you be "in the now"? There is only one Now. Nothing at all can enter the Now. It is the place of no thinking. In that space, there is only a realization of life energy and a sense of being. The Now is your connection to the universal life Source. It is often described as giving rise to a great feeling of peace or bliss, a sense of warmth or tingling in the body. Whether you laughed or cried a moment ago, those emotions do not exist in the here and now. There is no joy or sadness, no worry or anticipation. Nothing at all can squeeze itself into the time we call "Now" because it cannot be measured even in seconds. This is only being.

If you awaken to this moment, the here and now, then you will know that great peace is generated from a sense of being, and from a connection with the Tao. When you clearly understand and experience the Now, you can create your own happiness through your connection with the divine, your True Self.

The Now is the doorway into eternity. Those who know Now, know eternity. You cannot feel eternity if you fall into delusion and anguish over past or future. In this moment, cut off from past and future, you can encounter eternity in the here and now, a place that can't be measured by our concept of time. All realizations come to us in the here and now. Even conclusions reached after thinking intently about something for a long time actually come to us in an instant. The Tao is found in this moment, Now.

Many people are fearful, having lost the present and become entangled in past and future. Our souls must encounter eternity in the here and now in order to find stability. The true eternity we pursue is not only for after death, but for living while feeling eternity in each and every moment. Awakening to your being in the here and now every day, and realizing your existential value, allows you to feel eternity in this moment. Being in the Now enables us to hear that deep voice within. This voice is the inner guidance of our soul. When we tap into this divine intelligence, we are able to make clear choices and create the future of our dreams.

We can only choose in the moment of the Now. Both past and future exist in a place beyond the reach of our decisions. Our present choices create the future. So, if we lose the present, we have no future, either.

Our brains are performing their functions in this moment. Thus, to awaken to the Now is to awaken to your brain. Now is the only time when you can become the master of your brain. You can change information from the past and prepare for the future through your choices and actions now.

We meet new opportunities in each moment. Everything that we encountered in the past has no relationship to us now, in this moment. Nothing from the past can disturb the newness and sacredness of this moment, in the here and now. In each moment, we can begin anew.

> Awakening to your being in the here and now every day allows you to feel eternity in this moment.

Do you want change? Do you want to live a life that's different than the one you have lived thus far? If so, then begin now. Whoever you were up until a moment ago, whatever situation you faced, you can start anew now. Go back to the seat of self-existent life, which is without beginning and without end, and gain new strength. Begin the life you want to lead right now.

CHAPTER ELEVEN

The Brain and Enlightenment

IN CHAPTERS ONE THROUGH TEN OF THIS BOOK, you've traveled with me on a Tao journey for the completion of the soul. You've reflected on fundamental questions and issues of life, from human birth and death, to the eternal world of energy beyond it. I believe that our lives are themselves a journey of the soul for reaching the Tao. Although we came into this world empty-handed and will leave it empty-handed, if we have experienced growth and completion of the soul on this journey, our energy will be filled with spiritual abundance.

There is a precious companion who is always with you on your journey—your body. This body makes your journey more meaningful and valuable. Our bodies include an energy system called the chakras or Dahnjons. Once you know about this energy system, you will see that it is an amazing map that reveals cosmic wisdom for the completion of our souls. This is where the mystery of the Tao is hidden.

The principles and practices of Brain Education that I created to help people use their brains according to their highest values are deeply rooted in the Korean tradition of Tao. Understanding the energy system of the human body and using it for the completion of your soul is the key to unleashing your brain's limitless potential. That's why I want to tell you about the system for completion of the soul contained within the seven chakras, before delving into a discussion on the brain and enlightenment.

To understand the chakra system is to understand the system for completion of the soul. When that immense, comprehensive plan has entered your head, you will fully realize the importance of the brain and enlightenment.

Map for Completion of the Soul

I've summed up as follows the chakra energy system, based on the principles of completion of the soul and Chunhwa, that have come down to us from Korean Sundo. Humans can experience the three stages through three births. And in the chakras there are three gates and three palaces.

The first birth is the birth of the body, with which we are very familiar. After a fetus has grown in its mother's womb, it passes the first chakra and is born on this planet. The first chakra is named the "Earth Gate" because it is the portal through which humans come out onto the earth. The second chakra, which is located in the uterus, is called the "Earth Palace," meaning that this is where the fetus grows. A human's very first physical form is the sperm and egg, which are so small they can be seen only through a microscope. After these two single cells unite, cell division occurs, and the form of the fetus begins to take shape. This is the stage of the sperm and the egg.

> The energy system in our bodies is an amazing map that reveals cosmic wisdom for the completion of our souls.

After this new life has taken shape in the womb for nine months, a child emerges onto the human stage. In every human body, the first and second chakras control the energy of reproduction and sexuality, and, along with the third chakra, play a pivotal role in physical life and vitality. The third chakra is located in the solar plexus near the stomach, and it is the energy center that manages appetite, ambition, and personal power. Through the first, second, and third chakras, we learn how to appropriately control basic needs related to physical health, sex, money, and fame, as well as the emotions that stem from these. When our second chakra (also known as the lower Dahnjon) is filled with Jung energy through energy training, that energy passes the third chakra, rising to the middle Dahnjon (the fourth chakra), where it is converted into Ki energy.

The fourth chakra is known as the "Human Palace" because that it is where the energy of the soul dwells and grows. In this place, we develop basic traits for the growth of the soul (honesty, sincerity, responsibility, courtesy, truthfulness) and experience the evolutionary stages of love (Hyo, Choong, and Tao). Once the energy of the soul in the middle Dahnjon becomes clearer and matures in the Human Palace, it naturally rises upward.

At this time, the fifth chakra in the throat acts as a filter, allowing the cleansed and purified energy of the soul to pass. The fifth chakra is called the "Soul's Gate" because the energy of the soul passes through it. If the energy of the soul is to pass through this gate, it must become clearer and lighter. This is possible only when it has been freed from the attachments of emotion and ego. In the course of passing the fifth chakra, we learn how to let go of our attachments one at a time by realizing that life brings only suffering and impermanence. In order to transcend these limitations, we begin to yearn for Muah. When the energy of the soul is liberated from the attachments of the body through Muah, it may then pass through the Soul's Gate, the fifth chakra. This stage is the second birth, the birth of the soul.

After passing through the Soul's Gate, the energy of the soul continues to rise through the sixth chakra. Here, it encounters the energy of divinity in the brain, and the energies of the soul and divinity become one in the sixth chakra. This parallels the meeting of sperm and egg in the second chakra. Just as the sperm swims up to unite with the egg, the energy of the soul in the chest rises to the brain to achieve unity with the energy of divinity. In the same way that the sperm and egg develop into a child in the womb (the second chakra or Earth Palace), the energies of the soul and divinity grow and develop in the sixth chakra. For this reason, the sixth chakra is called "Heaven's Palace."

When the energy of the soul encounters the energy of divinity, the judgments and ideas of our egos disappear and we experience Muah, a state of pure consciousness that is filled with the life energy of the cosmos. This state, in the language of Korea's Sundo, is called *Shin In Hap Il*. Shin refers to the divine energy of the upper Dahnjon, and In is the human soul's Ki energy, located in the middle Dahnjon. Hap means "to join or unite," and Il means "one." Thus, the complete interpretation of Shin In Hap Il is, "The energies of the soul and divinity unite to become one," or, "God and humanity become one." When our souls encounter the energy of divinity and have become one with it, we realize that our true nature is of the divine, one with the Source of the universe.

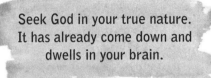

Seek God in your true nature. It has already come down and dwells in your brain.

The Shinhoon (literally, teachings on the divine) section of the *Sam Il Shin Go*, which, along with the Chun Bu Kyung, is one of Korea's three ancient scriptures, mentions this. It says "Seek God in your true nature. It has already come down and dwells in your brain." Amazingly, this text is thousands of years old, and it reveals the ancient wisdom that humanity already knows in its heart: Divinity already dwells in your brain, and this is your own true nature.

As with all human self-realization, enlightenment takes place in the brain, where it is realized and recognized. If you have experienced your sixth chakra, you may have a basic understanding of this phenomenon. This "third eye" may be awakened through breathing or meditation training. I have created a method called LifeParticle Meditation specifically to awaken the energy of this third-eye, the sixth chakra. Here, Ki energy is called "LifeParticles," which reflects quantum physics' understanding that energy can be simultaneously a particle and a wave, its perception depending on the consciousness of the observer.

These are phenomena that can be experienced through LifeParticle Meditation. After each of your lower chakras has awakened, the cleansed and purified energy rises to your head, activating the brain. When the energy in your brain is awakened and your third eye has opened, you will experience an indigo light in front of your forehead entering your brain like a whirlpool. When that mysterious indigo light rushes through your brain, your chest, and your entire body, all judgments and thoughts of the individualized self disappear. In that state, every cell in your body will tremble with ecstasy as you experience the great, unconditional love and life-sustaining energy of the cosmos.

Although that mysterious energy can be expressed using a variety of names, such as "deity," "the Source of the cosmos," and "the light of life," it is the same energy phenomenon that occurs when the Shin energy in the sixth chakra, the upper Dahnjon, awakens. It is the moment when the energy of our souls meets the energy of divinity and achieves unity in the brain. This is the moment of divine-human unity when we discover divinity within us, the moment the enlightenment of the Tao comes to us.

The Secret of Chunhwa

The secrets of Korean Sundo do not end here. The next stage, divine-human unity, is more important than anything.

When the divine energy of the sixth chakra is activated, it automatically awakens the energy of the seventh chakra, located at the top of your head. This awakening feels like the petals of a lotus flower opening. An energy line from the space above your head connects here and continues down like a beam of energy. The energy that comes into the crown of your head spreads out below in accordance with the chakra system, surrounding your body in the luminous energy of the cosmos and allowing you to feel complete integration and unity.

In Sundo, the crown chakra is called "Great Heaven's Gate," signifying that it is the gate for communion with heaven. Have you ever touched the crown of a baby's head? The crown of a baby's head is soft because the bones of a baby's skull are not yet connected. According to Sundo, the human soul enters the body of a fetus through this place. This is the main channel for the flow of cosmic energy, which maintains our lives and keeps us connected to heaven. That's why, since the ancient times of the Sundo culture, people were not allowed to haphazardly touch the crown of another person's head or to pass by the head of a person lying down. As the highest part of the human body and the part that is in touch with heaven, the crown of the head was the sacred portal through which a person received the energy of heaven. This shows the wisdom of the Sundo sages—and their careful maintenance of the energy line descend-

> The crown chakra is called "Great Heaven's Gate," the gate for communion with heaven.

ing from heaven into the crown of the head.

They also thought the crown of the head was important because it is the place where the completed soul leaves the body. The energy of the completed soul leaves the body through Great Heaven's Gate at the moment of death and returns to the Source of the universe, a process known in Sundo as Chunhwa, or the third birth.

Many sages who practiced Sundo in Korea refused to lie down at the moment of their deaths. They sat in the lotus posture, controlled their breathing, and experienced death in a state of oneness with the energy of the cosmos. They circulated energy through their bodies, opening wide Great Heaven's Gate so that their completed souls could leave through it. In the same way that the body of a child, completed in the Earth Palace, passes the first chakra to be born, the spiritual baby completed in Heaven's Palace is born through the seventh chakra. This is the completion of the soul, the secret of Chunhwa.

How to Activate the System of Soul Completion

Humans are said to be half-god and half-beast. In other words, we have an animal nature and a divine nature. The body's chakra system precisely reflects this fact. Of the seven chakras, the first, second, and third chakras control sexuality, appetite, and physical life energy, corresponding to the drives that other animals also have. The functions of these three chakras often flourish even more greatly in animals than in humans. Therefore, these three chakras alone are inadequate to describe the essence of human nature.

The fourth chakra, in the heart, is especially well developed in humans. However, it can also be felt in human-friendly animals, like dogs and horses, through the energy of the soul. The operation of the fifth chakra, which allows humans to empty themselves of attachments and to control their emotions, is also a human characteristic. Animals, on the other hand, usually express emotions like joy and anger without any sense of self-control. The sixth chakra, which lets humans experience unity with the energy of divinity, and the seventh chakra, which lets the completed soul be born anew, correspond to divine nature. In this way, a human's consciousness develops and grows from bestial to human, and then from human to divine as each chakra awakens.

Amazingly, the chakra system may be divided into upper and lower sections. Centered on the fourth chakra, it becomes precisely symmetrical, with the first, second, and third chakras below and the fifth, sixth, and seventh chakras above. The first chakra, the Earth Gate, and the seventh chakra, Heaven's Gate, are symmetrical. The second chakra, Earth Palace, and the sixth chakra, Heaven's Palace, are symmetrical. And the third chakra, through which Jung energy chang-

> The perfect energy system is innate in everyone's body, not just in special people.

es into Ki energy, and the fifth chakra, through which Ki energy changes into Shin energy, are symmetrical. If we say that the first and second chakras are a system for giving birth to the physical organism on the earth, then the sixth and seventh chakras are a system for giving birth to the soul in heaven in the world of cosmic energy.

Once you understand this system of spiritual completion, you will be truly amazed that it is built into the human body. This perfect system is innate in everyone's body, not just in special people. If the system were only in certain people, that would be unfair, but the impartial laws of the universe have installed the system in everyone. Actually, we are born into this world precisely for the purpose of activating this system of spiritual completion and to achieve Chunhwa. Unfortunately, few people know about this system, and even fewer know how to activate it, even if they do know of its existence.

What, then, should we do to activate the system of spiritual completion? To supply calories to the human body, you have to eat, and to supply it with oxygen, you have to inhale. In the same way, to activate the chakra system, you have to know the principles of its operation. Just as food and oxygen are the energy source for the physical system, Ki energy is the energy source for activating the chakra system. To put it another way, to activate your chakras, you have to do energy training. But the energy of your soul will not grow if you do energy training without any preparation. You have to know the fundamental principle behind energy generation. This principle is Shim Ki Hyul Jung, which means "energy follows where the mind goes."

The basic mechanisms underlying the energy of the chakra system are mind and consciousness. When you have a pure, mature consciousness, the energy of your soul also matures, and when you have bright consciousness, the energy of your divinity is illuminated. Mature, bright consciousness comes from a desire to seek the common good, not only your own private good. The ego's attachments to emotions and desires create murky, heavy, dark energy. Occasionally, there are people whose third eye opens and, believing they see the unseen world, they say, "I am a spiritual person." Even if your third eye opens, if the energy of your soul in your fourth chakra is attached to your ego, to your own selfish desires, your soul is not yet mature.

Not all energy is the same. There are differences in intensity, clarity, and brightness. I've given the name, "Cosmic Mind" (Chunjimaeum) to the pure consciousness that has awakened to the truth of the absolute selfless nature of things (Muah), and "Cosmic Energy" (Chunjikiun) to the pure life energy that comes out of the Cosmic Mind. The names themselves, however, are not important. What I want to emphasize is whether you truly feel that consciousness and energy.

> Our system of spiritual completion operates powerfully when we have pure cosmic mind and energy.

Our souls grow and our system of spiritual completion operates powerfully only when we have pure Cosmic Mind and are connected to Cosmic Energy. Doing good for the world through Cosmic Energy and Cosmic Mind is called "Hongik" in Korean. Through Hongik activities that share bright, pure mind and energy, our souls will grow, and a more harmonious, peaceful world will be created.

Five Steps of Brain Education

The heart of the realization of the Tao is achieving growth and completion of the soul by feeling and using pure energy (Cosmic Energy) in a selfless state of pure consciousness (Cosmic Mind). To traditional methods of energy training for this, like chakra and Dahnjon systems, I've added elements of modern brain science to create a newly devised method of Brain Education.

I've long felt that growth of consciousness and enlightenment should be available to everyone, not something attainable only through special spiritual exercises practiced while hidden away in the mountains. I feel that a scientific and popular approach is needed that allows anyone with a brain to experience them, and I have been researching these methods for many decades.

As a result, Brain Education was developed into an academic discipline and, through the University of Brain Education in Korea, masters and doctors of these disciplines are being born. What is more, the Korean Institute of Brain Science was established under the auspices of the Korean Ministry of Science and Technology, and it continues to conduct research on Brain Education. Additionally, I founded the International Brain Education Association (IBREA), which has special consultative status with the United Nations Economic and Social Council and is actively spreading Brain Education worldwide.

Brain Education divides the process of discovering your brain's latent potential and realizing your highest value into five main steps: 1) Brain Sensitizing, 2) Brain Versatilizing, 3) Brain Refreshing, 4) Brain Integrating, and 5) Brain Mastering.

These five steps offer a process for creating a productive, creative, and peaceful Power Brain, which is the goal of Brain Education. Each step is configured so that its contents match the structure, functions, and physiological characteristics of the brain. These steps begin in the body and continue, one step at a time, to activate the three-tiered structure of the brain. Ultimately, the program's goal is integration of the brain's three-tiered structure into a single whole.

We can divide our brain by function into three layers: the cerebral cortex, the limbic system, and the brain stem. Located on the very outside of the cerebrum, the cerebral cortex is called the "neocortex" because it is thought to be the part of the brain that developed last. It is also called the "human brain" because it is particularly well-developed in humans. The neocortex is the part that makes human behavior unique and allows us to remember, analyze, integrate, judge, and create based on language. Thus, the neocortex can also be called the "thinking brain."

Below the neocortex is the limbic system. The neocortex developed, at most, four million years ago, but the limbic system has been around for 200 million years. The limbic system developed in the course of mammalian evolution—in dogs, cattle, and horses, for example—and it manages motor nerves and a variety of emotional reactions, including fear, anger, and pleasure. The limbic system, which manages emotions like joy, anger, sorrow, and pleasure, can be called the "feeling brain."

At the very bottom of the brain's three levels is the brainstem. Neurologists speculate that it appeared when reptiles evolved approximately 500 million years ago. It is made up of the diencephalon, mesencephalon, myelencephalon, and pons. The brain stem generally performs autonomic nervous system functions essential to survival, such as respiration, circulation, digestion, and reproduction.

> Brain Education's goal is integration of the brain's three-tiered structure into a single whole.

These bodily functions operate continuously, without input from the conscious mind. What if we had to carefully manage every heartbeat, inhalation, and exhalation? Would that even be possible? The brain stem operates autonomously, without requiring orders from the neocortex, because it manages life directly. That's why the brain stem can be called the "life brain."

Step one, Brain Sensitizing, creates awareness of the body and entire brain. Step two, Brain Versatilizing, seeks to activate the functions of the neocortex. Step three, Brain Refreshing, alleviates the fixed concepts of the neocortex and clears negative emotional memories stored in the limbic system. Step four, Brain Integrating, unleashes the powers of the brain stem and reestablishes core values. Step five, Brain Mastering, maximizes use of the brain's functions for true mastery.

As you go through these five steps, you will awaken the infinite possibilities of your brain and will ultimately be able to use the functions of every part of your brain in an integrated way.

The following is a further description of the five steps of Brain Education:

Step 1: Brain Sensitizing

The first step of Brain Education begins with awakening your body's senses. Unlike other parts of our bodies, our brains are surrounded by a hard skull, and we can't touch or exercise them directly. However, our brains are made up of different domains for supervising each part of our bodies, and each part of our bodies and the relevant brain domains interact intimately with each other. Consequently, by moving our bodies and stimulating our senses, we can activate the relevant brain domains. You can feel and control the flow of energy in your body when its senses are sufficiently awakened, and your concentration increased. You can awaken your brain's senses much more efficiently if you use this energy sense.

Step 2: Brain Versatilizing

Viewed physically, the brain is one of the most flexible organs in our bodies. There are no bones or muscles in the brain. And although it seems soft at first glance, the brain is the organ with the most powerful resistance because of its fixed habits of thinking and believing. Habits and beliefs exist as circuits in the brain. The more repeatedly we use them, the more these circuits stabilize. Thanks to our brain's plasticity, though, we can always learn new things, and we can change old patterns of thinking and behavior. Brain Versatilizing is a course for stimulating neural circuits to make them flexible, and for getting out of our individual comfort zones to attempt new ways of thinking and acting. Through this process, you come to have a more flexible attitude and can approach challenges a little more creatively.

Step 3: Brain Refreshing

All of us accumulate an incredible amount of information in our brains. Some of that information contributes to our growth and development; much does not. What's important is the fact that information is merely information; it is not the substance of things. Brain Refreshing begins when you realize that you are the master of information, the one who searches for, revises, destroys, and creates it. In Brain Refreshing, you practice consciously releasing old, negative information that doesn't help you. In particular, you make your brain lighter and brighter by cleansing it of emotional memories that limit you. Through this process, your body and brain recover natural balance, and natural healing occurs as a result.

> Brain Integrating is the most important step for attaining the selfless state of Muah.

Step 4: Brain Integrating

As the most central course of the five steps of Brain Education, Brain Integrating, if we compare it to the process of Tao enlightenment, is the most important step for attaining the selfless state of Muah. You experience selflessness and feel your brain being integrated when the thoughts of your neocortex and the emotions of your limbic system quiet down and the life energy of your brain stem revives. Once your brain is integrated, you develop the power to achieve what you want through pure, clear consciousness and concentration. Brain Integrating is a process for re-examining your own belief system and reestablishing your core values, thereby reconfiguring the many areas of your life around your core values. When our thoughts, words, and deeds are one, and when our lives are consistent with what we truly want, we become able to use all the functions of our brains, including the creativity of the neocortex, the emotions of the limbic system, and the life force of the brain stem, in an integrated way. Then the many functions of the brain can cooperate and head toward a single goal, without going different directions.

Step 5: Brain Mastering

The final stage of Brain Education, rather than being a form of training as such, takes place through daily life. It corresponds to the Tao Study of Living. Mastering your brain means becoming able to use, to the greatest extent possible, the creativity of your integrated brain. In this step, you continue to live the productive, creative, peaceful life of a Power Brain by ceaselessly applying in your daily life the principles and methods for using your brain that you learned in the previous four steps. And, by realizing in your life the core values and concepts of self you discovered through Brain Integrating, you can work to practice Hongik, living and working for the good of all, and to achieve the growth of your consciousness.

Five Principles of Brain Operating System

I felt the need for simple behavioral guidelines that would facilitate ready application of the Five Steps of Brain Education in daily life. And I thought that, in the same way that computers have operating systems, we, as the masters of our brains, needed a system for operating our brains well. What I created was the Brain Operating System, or BOS. Here, I'll introduce five BOS principles for practicing Tao enlightenment in your daily life as the master of your brain.

The 1st BOS Principle: Pay Attention!

To pay attention means to be aware of your brain and concentrate on the "here and now." It is not living in the past, dominated by previous successes or misfortunes, nor is it living in the future, consumed by fantasies or fears. To pay attention means to face reality squarely, without illusions, and to enjoy each precious moment of life. It also means

> The five BOS principles are for practicing Tao enlightenment in your daily life as the master of your brain.

resolutely solving your problems within reality as you create your future. The reason people fail to live in the here and now is that their minds are not where they should be, but have rather drifted off somewhere else. Their minds may be focused on thoughts of the past or the future, on physical or spiritual objects, on dreams of prestige or power, or on other people.

So, where is your mind now? Is it encountering your brain and your life, or is it off thinking about things apart from you? Your mind will return to its proper place when you are conscious of your brain, which means you are conscious of your life.

Even if what you pursue is an outside object, you can concentrate on it while remaining consciously awakened to the life within you. This type of concentration is relaxed and calm, allowing you to observe yourself and your object through an integrated brain. Waking up and paying attention also means recovering your zero point and recovering your balance. The "zero point" is a balanced state that doesn't lean toward anything. You can make correct choices and judgments in that state.

If your mind is distracted by external objects, and struggles while lost in a rolling ocean of information, wake up and take back your brain. Ignite the light of life in your brain.

The 2nd BOS Principle: Good News Creates a Good Brain!

Our brains are exposed to a flood of information every day. Your brain receives endless reports through your five senses, from the time you open your eyes in the morning until you go to bed at night. It reads the newspaper, listens to the radio, watches TV, surfs the Internet, reads books, talks with colleagues, and listens to the conversation going on between people at the next table in the coffee shop. Before we can determine whether any of this information is true or not, or pertinent or not, it seeps into our subconscious mind and affects our thoughts, behaviors, and emotions.

Imagine you are eating really delicious food at a restaurant. What would you do if a restaurant employee suddenly came up to you and said, "I'm sorry. There is something inedible in your meal"? Even if what the employee said weren't true, on hearing his declaration, your brain would be shocked and would secrete stress hormones. That is the basic operation of the brain. The brain reacts and secretes hormones according to the information it receives, regardless of whether that information is factual. To get your brain to secrete hormones that are good for your body, you should provide your brain with positive information, making it feel good. Positive information makes the brain happy. Thus, the second principle: good news creates a good brain.

There is an interesting story related to this. An old Cherokee man sat his grandson down one day and said, "A good wolf and an evil wolf live in your heart, and the two are always fighting each other. Which wolf do you think will win?" The little boy thought about it for a while and asked his grandfather, "I don't know. Which wolf will win, Grandfather?" The old man's answer was simple: "Whichever one you feed."

> Which wolf is stronger inside you, the good wolf or the evil wolf?

Information in your brain, like the wolf, will grow stronger if you feed it. Feeding the good wolf means giving yourself good information and choosing the good information within you. Which wolf is stronger inside you, the good wolf or the evil wolf?

Examine your habits. Are the words you speak more positive or negative? If you have the habit of saying a lot of negative things in your everyday life, your overall life experience is likely to be more negative than positive. In this case, your brain has formed neural circuits that process information negatively. These circuits strengthen feelings of hurt and cut off any desire to take on a challenge.

When you have negative thoughts and emotions, it is easy to identify with those feelings and mistakenly believe that they are you. To prevent this, you must first be able to observe your inner thoughts, feelings, and emotions objectively. For example, when you're sad, say this to your brain as its master: "Hey, brain. You're sad right now. What can I do to comfort you?" Share with your brain messages containing love and encouragement. If you practice this, you'll come to realize that your emotions are not you, but yours. You will automatically be able to separate yourself from your emotions.

One of the best ways to enhance your positivity is to increase the amount of praise you give yourself and others. Don't become dispirited if others do not praise you much. Give yourself praise!

Often we have to develop the habit of giving praise before we can

 adequately receive it. We are all worthy of self-love and praise. Praising yourself acknowledges your divine essence and helps you develop confidence in yourself.

When confronted by a succession of difficulties, people think, "Why does this always happen to me?" But the more difficulties you face, the more strength you will develop over time. Pride and confidence are basic necessities for living a happy life. Once you lose trust in yourself, you will find it difficult to achieve anything of significance. So, the greater the difficulty you face, the more you need to encourage yourself with positive self-talk. Acknowledge even small accomplishments by repeatedly saying to yourself, "Yeah, you have done well" or "You are doing well" or "I can do this!" If you do this instead of dwelling on negative thoughts or self-defeating information, you will accomplish anything you set your mind to.

The 3rd BOS Principle: Choose and It Will Happen!

Our life, in short, is a series of choices. Nothing happens unless you make a choice. Let's imagine there is a little bell in front of you. Even though you know it is a bell, unless you strike it, it is nothing more than a lump of metal. The most important thing is action, or making the choice to strike it.

In the instant you choose, your brain is already starting to act. When you tell your brain, "I will do this!" it starts to create many situations that will allow you to realize that choice. The more intently you choose, and the longer you remain true to your choice, the more powerfully your brain reacts. Everything around you starts to change, new opportunities arise, and new encounters take place that support you in achieving that choice. You are simply manifesting in reality what has already been achieved in your brain.

> If you want something with all your heart, the universe aligns to make it happen.

This concept illustrates the principle of Shim Ki Hyul Jung, by which energy follows where the mind goes. If you want something with all your heart, the universe aligns to make it happen. It is not a matter of chance or probability. It's simply a matter of making up your mind, choosing within your heart, and opening up the world around you.

If you wanted something and couldn't achieve it, examine two things carefully and honestly. First, did you really want it earnestly, with all your heart? Second, did you use 100 percent of your energy to achieve it? To use all of your energy means to make use of your entire brain, not just a portion of it.

Think about what you want, feel the emotion of having it, and visualize yourself doing it. In this way, you use your entire brain and integrate the powerful forces that lie within it. When your brain is integrated, magical things begin to happen. Complicated thoughts, unstable fears, and negative information cease to exist. Your store of confidence and your belief in yourself rise to unwavering heights. Your creative potential, previously latent and deep within your brain, ignites, and you realize your dreams.

In addition to choosing, you must act with persistence and determination. Whenever you encounter obstacles, you must choose again and again without giving up. Soon, new solutions will present themselves. If you hold fast to your dream and develop trust in your creative potential, it will one day become your reality.

The 4th BOS Principle: Master Time and Space!

While on this earthly plane, we always live in time and space. Being aware that you're living in time and space means that you're living as the master of those things. People generally tend to live lost in their own emotions and desires, or they become preoccupied by trivial events without being aware of space and time. That gradually leads them to view themselves as small, weak beings and to live dominated by time and space. Are you living now as the master of your time and space, or are you living ruled by them?

People controlled by time generally think they can't do this or that because they have no time. "I'm so busy," they lament. "I have no extra time in my life." These people should examine their habits to see whether they're truly using their time well. Mastering time means using time as efficiently as possible. You must be productive and creative to increase the efficiency of your time use. The condition of your body and mind is the basis for this. Those who look and rush unconditionally forward when their energy is depleted and who are filled with tangled thoughts and emotions are unlikely to create efficiently. Your body should have sufficient energy and vitality, and it's important for you to maximize your concentration on the work you're doing by emptying your mind of tangled thoughts and emotions. Genuine creativity revives when you can concentrate in a state of selflessness, in a zero-point state in which your thoughts and emotions have vanished and you are balanced.

When your creativity revives, your efficiency will improve so much that you'll be able to do, in just a few dozen minutes, work that would normally take several hours. Because you will be dealing with things in a speedy way with lucid judgment, creative ideas and solutions will pour out of you. In such moments, your brain will fill with the joy of creation. Through this sense of achievement, you confirm your own life and existential value.

People who have mastered time not only manage their own time efficiently, but they also remember to devote some time to their own management and self-cultivation. They know that getting themselves in good condition physically and mentally is a shortcut that allows them to use their time more efficiently and productively. In such people, we do not feel a frantic busyness created by work that has driven them to forget themselves completely. Instead, we sense an unshakable centeredness that allows them to have the composure to handle work efficiently with a smile and with passion for life.

> Mastering time means using time as efficiently and productively as possible.

There are two kinds of people who are ruled by space. The first are people who are bound to the environment in which they belong, spinning in circles and living only within its limits. To such people, I recommend getting away from a gerbil-wheel life and going to a new place. Attending a meditation tour in search of yourself would be a good opportunity that would allow you to refresh your brain and encounter your inner world. Ideally, prepare well and leave on the trip for a few days, but if that's not possible, find a place nearby where you can recharge your body and mind. For example, you could find a yoga studio, a walking trail, or even a tree you can lean against. It helps to find "my spot"—a place where you can set aside your chaotic thoughts, even if only for a moment, and encounter your inner world.

The second kind of people who are controlled by space are those who are not satisfied with the place where they currently find themselves. They think, "I want to work (or live) some-where other than here." We tend to dream of new places when our repetitive lives become tiresome or troublesome. Would your happiness be guaranteed by moving to a new job or a new city? Perhaps it could, but unless your thought patterns and habits change, before long you might end up longing for yet another new place. Although finding where you belong is important, more important is discovering and realizing some meaning or value in that space.

If you want to become the master of your time and space, you must first precisely establish the meaning of your existence. Try reflecting on the question, "Why am I living now, in this time and space?" In other words, find the purpose and meaning of your life. If you have a dream you want to realize, it will grant significance to the space and time surrounding you, and you'll be able to visualize yourself firmly centered within them. By becoming the master of that space and time, instead of being led about by them, you will be able to live a creative life.

The 5th BOS Principle: Design All Your Environments!

Many environments make up the surroundings of your life: your living spaces, like your home and workplace; the people around you, like your friends, family, and colleagues; the work you do and the hobbies you pursue; and even your own body and mind.

We always hope to live in good environments, but there's no guarantee that we will. It's a universal truth of life and the cosmos that environment is variable. You never know when a bad situation will come to someone living in a good environment. Sometimes, people who have been living only in good environments give up more easily than others when confronted by a difficult situations. In contrast, there are people who change their environments as they want, even though they may have started in a bad environment. Many of the people who have been successful in the world were not handed good environments by their parents, but they instead overcame these difficult environments.

> If your soul awakens, you become able to redesign your enviroment instead of being ruled by it.

Live for a while and you find that life is not all clear days and sunshine. It might rain, it might snow, and the wind might blow. Unhappiness and happiness can come in anyone's life. You might get sick, or the people you care for might get sick. Although there are times when you feel great joy and happiness, there are also times when you feel lonely, sad, and angry. It is normal for such emotions to arise as our environments change, because we prefer stable environments. You should realize, though, that such emotions are themselves a kind of environment. And, as the master of any environment, you must be able to watch your emotions objectively as you experience environmental change.

The ultimate master of our environments is our consciousness, our soul. It is our soul that can shine brightly, even before death— and death can be called the most serious change of environment in the whole of life. If your soul awakens, you become able to use and redesign your environment instead of being ruled by it. This means you are able to change unhappiness into happiness and adversity into hope. The power of your soul manifests when you gladly accept the environment you've been given as the subject of study for the growth of your soul, and as an issue you should solve in your current lifetime.

If, instead of despairing or lamenting over your environment, you make up your mind to *love your life* no matter what environment you've been given, in that moment, amazingly, your negative consciousness will be changed into positive consciousness. And when, through sustained spiritual practice, you begin to change your internal environment—your body and mind—into something healthy and vigorous, the power of your soul will gain even more resiliency.

You should also remember that you participate in other people's environments, as well. You can choose to be a good or bad environment for that person. It is your consciousness, the power of your soul, that makes this choice. When you share bright energy with those around you in the hope that all of them—your family, friends, colleagues, and everyone around you—will become happier, you become a beneficial and reliable environment for them.

Viewed from a broader perspective, even the situations faced by the communities or countries to which we belong, including the human race and the earth, are important environments influencing us. As time goes on, countless people are losing hope amid increasingly fierce competition to survive. In such an environment, though you live but a day, how, through an awakened consciousness, will you live a life that contributes to the energy field of the whole?

Those who create a positive environment for themselves also create a positive environment for everyone. Your brain is the greatest tool that you have to create the life you want, complete your soul, and live a life of Tao. Cherish your brain and use it well.

CHAPTER TWELVE

Dreaming of a Tao World

HOW HAS YOUR TAO JOURNEY WITH ME BEEN SO FAR? I'm sure it's brought some awakenings if you've started to see your life and the world through Tao eyes. The subject we will address in this last chapter is how, united as one, we can transcend our small selves to create a better world. In other words, I will discuss how to apply the principles of the Tao to this world in which we coexist.

For this, we must first look back on the mark humanity has left so far. The human species has been developing diverse spiritual cultures and material civilizations based on its intellect, reason, creativity, and inspiration.

Although there are different perspectives for interpreting human history, here I intend to address important changes in the relationship between humanity and divinity. Why? Because changes in human consciousness have played a crucial role in pulling forward the development of human history, and because when we speak of human consciousness, it is a subject from which we can never exclude divinity. When we reflect on the history of humankind based on the relationship of the human with the divine, we can see that two general ages capture the essence of its development.

Two Ages of Humanity

In primeval times, humans were feeble creatures. Humans, who have relatively docile natures compared with other fierce, violent animals, were cast into nature, and they had to survive somehow. Using their intellect, they learned over time how to fashion tools, farm, and survive in the natural world. Floods, famine, earthquakes, volcanic eruptions, and other such natural phenomena were terrifying threats to human survival and completely beyond human control. These ancient people, who didn't understand the principles by which these natural phenomena occur, thought they happened because the gods were angry. Since that time, humans have been longing for divine blessings and protection, which they've sought to obtain by obeying and worshiping gods.

Humanity's worries didn't end there, though. Our powerful mental capabilities allowed us to contemplate our own existence in ways that other animals cannot. Who am I? Why are humans born; why do they grow old, get sick, and die? What is life after death like? How were nature and humanity created, and what power rules this world? The human species has worked continuously to solve such riddles about human identity and the essence of the universe. To this end, our ancestors started to organize and develop those questions and answers

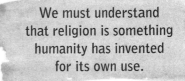

We must understand that religion is something humanity has invented for its own use.

in the form of religion. They thought there probably existed, in a dimension different from that of humans, and in a domain that human power fails to reach, a being beyond the scope of human reason. To that being they gave the name God. And they sought to gain comfort and peace of mind by obeying, relying on, and praying to this God who controls all creation.

Such was the thinking of the God-centered era. It was a time when people thought that gods were the center and subjects of the world, and humans were merely creatures subordinate to them. Because gods were the focal point of this age, society naturally focused on the religions that served them, and many religions were born and flourished in countless regions and among many peoples on the earth.

We must clearly understand, however, that religion is not the truth of nature itself, but rather is something humanity has invented for its own use. Organized and politicized by humans, religions have mass-produced countless problems. Various religions and many religious leaders have acted as though God is on their side, and not on the side of their enemies. They've engaged in numerous forms of corruption in the name of God and have even justified violence and murder through religious war. Inter-religious conflict and confrontation, which stem from religious group self-ishness, have given rise to much bloodshed and death. This is true even today, as religious zealotry continues to threaten world peace and global stability.

This relationship between humans and the divine started to change as society went through the Renaissance and Enlighten-ment. Beginning in the fourteenth century, when corruption of reli-gion had reached an extreme, human reason slowly raised its head following a backlash against narrow medieval religious thought and the rigidity of tradition. The new value of humanism appeared, placing greater importance on humanity and experience. This pe-riod was called the Renaissance.

The Renaissance brought rapid change to the world of science and to the development of human values thanks to the formulation heliocentric theory, the invention of the printing press, and the na-vel exploration of the globe. In addition, the period saw an explo-sion of innovative artistic activities like those of Michelangelo and Leonardo da Vinci. As this spirit of the Renaissance spread to the church, fierce criticism of the medieval Church's materialism and worldliness started to rise.

Since then, the interest of most people has moved to the well-being of humanity as a whole. As Pythagoras said, "Man is the measure of all things." People have been working to make human life richer and more convenient through the gifts of human intellect and reason. As a result, humanity has achieved brilliant technological development and material abundance, and now it is picking up the pace of its efforts to explore the universe, once considered the Unknown.

However, clouds already darken the horizon of humanity's future. Although we hopefully imagine the brilliant technologies future civilization will bring, we are now having to face the imbalances that come with these marvels. The problem of the global environment now wraps its hands tightly around the throat of humanity's progress. Automobiles created to satisfy humanity's desire to move faster belch greenhouse gases; factories built to produce more, and more easily, have initiated a dangerous process of global warming. As a result, ice and glaciers at the Arctic and in Greenland are melting rapidly and have caused sea levels to rise fifteen to twenty centimeters over the past 100 years. El Niño, heat waves, cold waves, floods, and many other forms of unusual weather are occurring more frequently.

> Clouds already darken the horizen of humanity's future before we imagine the technologies it will bring.

Along with global warming, tropical forests, which are massive biological storehouses where half the earth's organisms live, have been reduced by half due to reckless deforestation. One-third of the planet is already desert or undergoing desertification, and half of the earth is expected to become a desert by 2100. More than a billion of the world's people are currently suffering from shortages of food and water. The United Nations predicts that in 2025, three billion people, 40% of the world's population, will face fresh water shortages. What's more, the World Wildlife Fund (WWF), in its 2012 Living Planet Report, stated that since the 1970s, biological diversity has decreased approximately 28% globally and dropped precipitously, by about 60%, in tropical regions. It further predicts that if things continue in this way, one-fourth of all living species will disappear by 2050. The report also states, based on 2008 figures, that current human resource consumption can only be sustained if we miraculously manifest 1.5 planets and that, unless we reduce resource consumption, we will need two planets by 2030 and three by 2050.

Among elements threatening humanity's survival, there are other problems we cannot overlook. One is infectious disease, a counterattack of microbes that includes everything from ordi- nary colds and flu to polio, AIDS, and Ebola. We can easily imagine the worst-case scenario—some new, airborne infectious disease appearing and driving humanity into a terrifying state. And nuclear power, which was developed for human convenience, could push humanity down the path of self-destruction and self-annihilation if global relations take the darkest turn, because these weapons have enough destructive power to swallow up all humankind and most living things on Earth.

And yet another problem lies in wait, one that is every bit as serious as the crisis situations facing humankind listed above. It is a loss of humanity. Increasing rates of depression, drug addiction, and suicide show one aspect of it. The materialism prevalent worldwide has brought a confusion of values and a loss of morality, and it is leading to mass alienation by causing estrangement between people, even among family members.

In this way, the humanism that has created human civilization over the past several centuries, a culture that exalted human rationality and reason, is also vividly revealing its limitations. Humans have reveled in freedom and pleasure apart from divinity for a while now. As the bedrock of human culture has moved from God-centered to human-centered values, somewhere deep within, people have remained troubled by confusion and emptiness. Although humanism brought material abundance, it created a wasteland of human spirit; it has brought sickness to the air, water, and nature, the resources upon which human life depends.

It is now time for us to directly face the limits of God-centered and human-centered outlooks.

It is now time for us to directly face these limits, revealed in the history of our species, of God-centered and human-centered outlooks. Through straightforward examination of this kind, we will begin to find possible solutions.

If we retrace humanity's steps, we can see that the history of the species has ultimately been one of longing and yearning for the essence of life, the world, and the universe—in other words, of a deep desire to know the Tao. Through one—God-centeredness—we spiritually approached the divine and the Unknown; through the other—human-centeredness—we used human reason and intellect to solve the riddles of the Unknown.

Both of these perspectives have a problem: they perceive humanity and divinity, human and nature, subject and object as separate. The God-centered perspective viewed the divine and human as separate things—God as master and human as slave—so humans were seen as fallen beings who always had to obey and pray to the divine. The human-centered perspective viewed humanity as subject and nature as object, separate from humankind, so nature became something that humanity should always conquer.

The problem stems from the kind of thinking that always classifies and separates everything into self and God, self and others, and self and nature. The key to solving the problem, then, is very clear. Humanity needs an integrated way of thinking that views all things as one. In other words, it is a way of thinking that, by recovering divinity within humanity, perceives humanity and divinity as one, and that realizes that humankind is not separate from nature, but a part of it.

What is the secret that will allow us to integrate our vision? The secret is found in energy, a point I have stressed frequently throughout this book. Energy is the medium that flows through and interconnects everything in the world, the visible material world along with the unseen world of consciousness. The answers we seek exist in the life energy of nature and the cosmos, and in the principles and laws by which that energy operates—in other words, in the principles of the Tao.

The True God

There are two kinds of things we call God. One is the god arising from the belief systems we call religions. The gods of certain regions and of certain ethnic groups haves dominated human consciousness until now. These gods are actually nothing more than forms of information created by humans that only live when they are maintained by human belief.

The other type of deity is one that cannot be shackled or limited within the confines of any particular religion and that cannot be defined using knowledge or ideas. This God was not created by humanity, but is nature itself. It is the unseen life energy operating nature and the universe, a force that existed long before the concept of divinity ever arose in the consciousness of the human race. It is also the laws of that energy, the world of the Tao.

Humans have created a being to govern natural phenomena that are beyond the understanding of the rational brain, and to help them understand the mysteries of life that are indescribable in human language. They have named this being God. But in fact, that God is not a certain being, but the law of the infinite life energy of the cosmos. In that law, there are no artificial intentions, emotions, or distortions. It merely operates with disinterest according to the laws of energy, like water flowing downhill. Some might ask who created that energy and those laws. They were not created by any certain being. They are self-existent.

> The true God was not created by humanity, but is nature itself, the laws of life energy, the world of the Tao.

Some might ask, then, when those laws began to exist. The concept of time in the world of the Tao, however, exists beyond our concept of time. It is without beginning and without end. The great life force of the cosmos is eternally self-existent, without beginning and without end; this is the world of the Tao.

True divinity has no form. If it has form, it isn't God. Why? Because God is the life energy of nature and the cosmos, the law of the universe itself. God is not some image or idea humanity has created. The most powerful idols we should guard against are erroneous ideas and images of God. The true God does not exist as an image or idea. If you're still curious about God's form, then we can say it is nature itself, where the life energy of the universe operates without beginning and without end.

The true God has no emotions. Many religions have imagined God as a being who bestows love and blessings upon those who believe in him and wrath and curses upon those who do not. These are not God's true attributes. Such emotions are merely attributes of humanity. For the interests of religious groups, the properties of the divine have been manipulated down to the level of childish human emotions so that they are characterized by envy, anger, jealousy, and even damnation. The true God is not a personified deity who blesses those who believe in him and punishes those who do not. God exists as impartial law, not as a person. If you put your hand in boiling water, you'll get burned. It's a law. Not putting your hand in boiling water is respecting the law. Praying to God to keep you from being burned as you stick your hand in hot water is foolishness.

The true God does not seek to rule anyone or to be worshiped by anyone. If God wanted to be worshiped and glorified, it would be proof that he was imperfect and lacked something. The true God is the law of life energy itself, which, in this very moment, causes the earth to turn and our hearts to beat, even though we don't glorify it. There is nothing else God wants, because it already exists in everything in the universe. If God were to demand anything, it would be that we show love toward our neighbors and the world. The sun gives its light fairly to everyone, without demanding anything in return, to believer and nonbeliever alike. The earth, too, supplies us with water and air, but doesn't demand anything as payment. All we have to do is feel the love of the sun and the earth, and love each other with that same abundant love.

Genuine truth frees the soul. Religion itself, however, does not make the soul free. People's souls are fettered and their divine natures dimmed by narrow-minded religious customs and dogma.

Religion must not be a curtain that hides the true God, the light of the great life of the cosmos. You must be freed from all attachments if your soul is to be liberated, so religion must not be another attachment.

There is a saying in the East: "On the Great Way, there are no gates." This means that although countless gates may exist that lead to small paths in the form of religion or philosophy or art, no specific frameworks or signs are needed to reach the Great Way. To put it another way, in attaining the Great Way there are no limiting structures or provisions that say, "You can be saved only through this religion. You can go to heaven only if you believe in this person." Regardless of whether you believe in religion, by becoming one with the great life energy of the cosmos, you can reach the world of the great Tao.

> By becoming one with the great life energy of the cosmos, you can reach the world of the great Tao.

The Third Age

When you meet the life energy of the Tao, your soul opens its eyes and your divine nature is illuminated. You feel the energy of infinite love, peace, and blessing in a selfless state of Muah, which is not attached to or bound by anything, surrounds your whole body and vibrates and blows life force into your cells. We can most easily feel that blessing within the beating of our hearts, which beat without resting for even a moment. You have never lacked the love and blessings of life energy, not even for a moment. If it feels otherwise, you simply haven't realized it is there for you. Unless you realize it, your mind will remain lonely and sad, and your body will easily become sick.

It is now time for everyone to become one with the life energy of the cosmos and to seek his or her soul and divinity. Since everyone has a soul and a divine nature, each of us should definitely know how to realize this and make good use of them. Very few schools in this world, however, teach about the substance of the soul and divine nature. Most people have been teaching these things using religious methods, which misses the mark. Instead of realizing their divinity, people have been busy worshipping gods, repenting their wrongs to those gods, and imploring those gods to give them what they want. We must now find the God who actually exists in life, not some conceptual god created by human beings. If you turn your outward-looking eyes inward, and search for God in the original nature within you, you'll find that this spirit has already descended and dwells in your brain. We need to have a realization about the divinity that is living and breathing in our lives, not God as an object separate from humanity.

The age of a new dimension that overcomes the limits of human consciousness will begin with such a spiritual realization by humanity. The human species will welcome a new third age after it has overcome the limitations of the god-centered and human-centered ages, which still influence life on this planet. The era of divine-human unity will be led by people who have realized the divine nature within themselves. In other words, it will be a time during which divinity has awakened in humanity, a time when God and humanity are one.

People who have awakened to their divine nature will be able to see with an integrated consciousness that humanity and divinity, humanity and nature, and matter and spirit are one. They will come to have a new identity that integrates divinity and humanity, individuality and totality. Humans in the era of divine-human unity will be leaders of harmony, capable of connecting dualistic, separate poles and overcoming all confrontation and conflict. And, by knowing that our Source is one, they will come to have a bright, lofty consciousness that leaps beyond all artificial categories and distinctions created by ethnicity, ideology, and religion. Creators of harmony and peace: this is the true image of humanity in a new age.

The age of divine-human unity is a time when the brain awakens. It is a time when the brains of humans who were once in darkness awaken, automatically coming to know the principles of the cosmos and nature, the principles of the Tao. When the divine Shin energy in the brain is illuminated, we will enter the Era of Enlightenment, also called the Shinmyung Era. If you awaken to the true identity of humanity, without any need to blindly believe in something, your divinity will automatically be illuminated, and you will come to know the truth of the Tao. In this era, knowing that divinity is found in the human brain, and that humanity's true identity is divinity, will be common knowledge. And people will use their divinity to shine light on the world as true creators. This era of divine-human unity is a time for *using* divinity, not a time for serving God.

> The human species will welcome a new third age, the era of divine-humanity unity.

The Era of Shinmyung is a world in which the mystery of the Tao is fully revealed. The current world is filled with mystery. So far, though, we have only observed that mystery; we've never been able to enter into it. In other words, we've failed to become participants in that mysterious world. We have been mired in narrow information and ideas, and we have just been staring at the mystery. But when humans' divinity is illuminated, everyone will open their Tao eyes, their eyes of truth, and come to see and judge the world through truth. Then everything that had been all mixed up and confused will find its proper place. We are directly connected with the mysterious world, with the information of the universe and, by using that energy, we become able to easily find solutions to physical and spiritual problems.

Conversely, the number of narrow-minded people who are trapped in dualistic worldviews and who promote confrontation and conflict will decline. They will be considered backward and outdated. Lies work when people don't know that they are lies. The true Era of Shinmyung, the time of divine-human unity, is a world in which the consciousness of people has become so bright that falsehood and manipulation no longer work.

The era of divine-human unity means that the true Era of Spiritual Civilization has come. In the Era of Material Civilization, matter became the central value, dominating and ruling people's spirits. In the Era of Spiritual Civilization, spiritual values will take center stage. This doesn't mean that people will exclude or deny matter. Instead, awakened people will *use* matter for realizing spiritual values. Instead of being the goal itself, matter will be a tool for the growth of consciousness and for creating the world of the Tao.

The spiritual civilization is a mature civilization that embraces the useful, sustainable products of material civilization while overcoming their limitations. In this civilization, people who have awakened to the laws of nature and the principle of harmony will spontaneously and naturally create a sustainable world, rather than by force. If material civilization developed external power, then spiritual civilization develops internal power. That power is harmony, reconciliation, forgiveness, love, and peace.

Until now, human civilization has continuously been inhaling only, seeking to possess more and accumulate more. If you breathe in, sooner or later you have to breathe out. It's a law of natural life and a law of the Tao. The cycle of breathing, which takes place through the repetitive rhythm of inhalation and exhalation, expansion and contraction, is a natural rhythm of life that happens automatically, like a natural instinct. The current way of life among the human species, however, goes against this self-evident principle of nature, and the result is the situation that humanity and the earth now face. This means that, whether we like it or not, humanity has to change the direction its boat is traveling. It's now time for humanity to change from inhaling to exhaling, and comply with the laws of nature and the principles of the Tao.

> It's now time for humanity to change from inhaling to exhaling, and comply with the laws of nature.

Breathing out means realizing that the attachments you've been holding onto are, in fact, impermanent and a source of suffering. And it means forgiving and reconciling relationships with each other and heading forward toward genuine peace. Peace is a problem of circulation. Even now, on one side of the planet, there is so much food that it gets discarded, while on the other side, many people are starving to death because they don't have anything to eat. This is because the circulation of food, of energy, and of love is not happening as well as it should. If we abandon our attachments to our desires, give up our consciousness of separation and discrimination, and go back to the life of nature itself, we will be able to integrate with each other and have true reconciliation and oneness.

This era will ultimately become possible through the circulation of information. Information of enlightenment that shatters outdated concepts will have to be circulated rapidly. To that end, people and organizations with enlightened consciousness will have to provide information as they engage in vigorous activity. In this sense, I see hope in material civilization. This is because, thanks to the development of TV, the Internet, and mobile communications, the transmission of information has become incomparably faster than in the past. I believe that the speed of transmission will increase exponentially once human consciousness starts to perceive the common values our species should pursue.

Will we continue only to inhale, or will we exhale? The choice is ours. Will you keep breathing in without ever stopping, or will you exhale comfortably? The future of our species depends on us humans. The Era of Spiritual Civilization will come to this land when the cycle of human civilization changes from inhaling to exhaling, from a paradigm of competition and control to a paradigm of harmony and reconciliation.

Central Values of Human Community

What then should be the central value to guide this peaceful global village? Humanity currently faces a crisis of civilization and needs a centripetal point to end any further confrontation and to pull it back from infinite competition. Without new values that humans can pursue jointly, we will inevitably continue our tumble down the path of strife, conflict, and mutual destruction. These new values must clearly benefit all humans existing on the planet, not certain individuals or groups. The greatest and most central value on the planet with which all humanity can agree is the earth itself.

Humanity hasn't yet been able to understand the true meaning of the earth as a central value because the planet is too large compared to the range of things we can perceive and experience. Because it is so large and close, we have not been able to perceive it, like a fish that isn't aware of the water's existence. Fish that fight and compete with other fish for food consider only the food in front of their eyes to be the source of their lives. Even though the ocean that contains their bodies is the source of their existence, they can't feel it because it is so massive and so close. This also applies to humans. We consider absolute the values that we believe maintain us and, as we compete and struggle with each other over these things, we live forgetting the most important value that is the basis of our lives.

> The greatest and most central value on the planet with which all humanity can agree is the earth itself.

The largest whole on the planet is neither a people nor a nation, but the earth itself. The key opening the way to a peaceful Earth Village is a shift to an understanding that views the earth as the center of all values. This is because, once we properly understand the existence and meaning of the earth, it becomes clear to us that what we have believed were absolute values are nothing more than relative values.

We can say that the countless conflicts tainting human history are the results of conflicts between relative values seeking to rise to the status of absolute value. The results are the same even if the value proclaimed is "peace." We have to look at what that peace is centered on. Efforts at peace focused on one religion or one country cannot help but conflict with each other. Those behind these efforts are centered on different things, so they clash and fight with each other over the version of peace that each wants. A true foundation for world peace will finally be formed when we perceive the earth as our central value and respect each other from the position that all nations, religions, and ideologies are relative values.

There is another important, central value, in addition to the earth. It is "humanity." To put it more precisely, it is human consciousness, the human brain. For humankind can be connected as one consciousness through the brain. The Era of Spiritual Civilization begins with a realization concerning the brain. We have to recover our brains from anachronistic information that has taken hold of us. As long as we rely on conceptual information for our identities, we will be nothing more than Indians or Americans or Koreans, or nothing more than Christians or Buddhists or Hindus.

The common identity of humans living on our blue Earth is only "Earth Citizens." Countless people have come to the earth and, unaware even of the fact that they are Earth Citizens, have left this planet without gaining much. We have to escape from outdated conceptual information and recover our true identity. Letting your brain be dominated by ideas that have flowed in from the outside is just like turning on your computer and then leaving it that way while, in your absence, someone else uses it in whatever way they want.

Who is the master of your brain? And what does your brain ultimately want? The brain fundamentally pursues peace. If you go deep inside, riding on the rhythm of life, you can encounter a world of peace, the world of selflessness (Muah) in a place beyond doubt, fear, thought, judgment, emotion, and memory. In the moment you realize that all is one, infinite love and responsibility for all things and humanity arise in you. You come to pursue a peace that benefits everyone and brings life to the planet and all humanity, rather than a peace that benefits a specific individual or group.

Humanity and the earth are central values of peace that embrace all and integrate what is separated. The only objects we should truly love, the objects we should defend even at the risk of our lives, are humanity and the earth. Love for humanity and love for the earth! These are keys opening the way to the peaceful era of the global village in the twenty-first century.

Finding Our Lost Nature

The world we see with our open Tao eyes is a single world interconnected by cosmic life energy. Feeling nature is the easiest way to feel the truth of the Tao.

I live in Sedona, Arizona, which is surrounded by red earth and rocks and green cactus and junipers. I came to know Sedona twenty years ago. It was then that I visited and explored all of Sedona's hidden places and was intoxicated by its powerful and mysterious allure. I

> Humanity and the earth are central values of peace that embrace all and integrate what is separated.

was repeatedly struck by wonder and said to myself, "Sedona is truly beautiful." I thought I was seeing Sedona.

But in that moment I realized that Sedona was watching me. Before I was watching Sedona, Sedona's red rocks, cactuses, and juniper trees were watching me. They existed in that place long before I did, and they had been watching countless people come and go. And they will continue to silently watch over this land after we humans are gone. So they, the elements of nature, are the true masters of this land.

After I had switched from the perception that I was watching Sedona to the understanding that Sedona was watching me, I had another realization. It was that I am also "nature itself," existing within the flow of infinite life energy. It's easy for me to feel that I am a human and thus separate from nature because of artificial knowledge and ideas. I can feel that I, too, am a part of that nature once I set aside preconceptions and simply feel myself in nature. With my heart beating inside me as I breathed the life energy of nature, I realized that I am not man-made, but that I am nature itself. And, as a part of nature, I am interconnected with everything in the life energy field of the whole. Self and nature, subject and object, spirit and matter are not separate things but are moving as waves, united in that massive life-energy field.

The Chun Bu Kyung says this about such a realization: "In Joong Chun Ji Il." This means that heaven and earth are one in humanity. Here, heaven (Chun) is unseen energy and consciousness, and earth (Ji) is visible matter, but heaven and earth ultimately mean nature. When people understand that humans have nature inside of them, and that they are, ultimately, nature itself, we humans (In) will awaken to the one (Il) that exists without beginning or end, which is the main message of the Chun Bu Kyung.

Those who realize that they are one with nature come to *feel* automatically that we are all interconnected within the great expanse of life energy. After this realization, the thick wall of ideas and ego that causes us to perceive ourselves as beings separate from each other begins to break down.

Knowing that I am nature, and feeling oneness within it—this is ultimate enlightenment of the Tao. It's about each of us becoming one with nature and realizing a world of genuine harmony and peace. This is the world of the Tao of which I dream. It is also probably the world you who are reading this book, and many people with awakened consciousness, dream of.

There is a story that is a worthy model for us who long for this world. It comes from the book *Bu Do Ji* written by the scholar Park Jesang, who lived during Korea's Silla Period.

Long, long ago, a community called Mago Castle was established by Mago, Mother Earth, in the highest and most sacred land on the planet. The people of Mago Castle lived in harmony with nature. This community operated autonomously, based on the sense of harmony in all people, not according to some higher authority or artificial rules. They had a deep sense of connection and oneness with other living things. Though all acted freely, each in his or her own way, they didn't harm others and enjoyed order and peace.

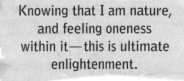
Knowing that I am nature, and feeling oneness within it—this is ultimate enlightenment.

They lived on the milk of the earth, Jiyu, which is the vital energy of the ground. Then, one day, someone ate grapes and discovered the five senses and the ego. As gradually more of them consumed other living things, the people of Mago Castle lost their absolute unity with other beings, their original purity, and their connection with nature. A battle and struggle over resources began, and their self-control vanished, eventually shattering the harmony and order of Mago Castle.

Their tribal leaders understood they could no longer remain there as they were, and they chose to lead all the people away in an exodus to protect their precious Mago Castle. They vowed to recover their lost true nature and return one day to Mago Castle. This is the Vow of Bokbon (Recovring one's true nature).

I was deeply moved and impressed by this story. The story of Mago Castle is a beautiful symbolic myth illustrating self-discovery, honest introspection, and the brave journey of the human spirit. This story shows us what humanity, deep down, actually aims to become and where it seeks to return.

I often say that true enlightenment is realizing this statement: "I am a human and nature itself." What makes us truly human is not money or profound knowledge or advanced technology. Rather, it is the sense of harmony and peace inside us that arises from the realization that we are nature itself. It is also the heart that, when this sense awakens, empowers us to treat other people and life with understanding, respect, and love. This is the autonomy, the essence of the human spirit, and our true nature, which we find in the story of Mago Castle.

The problems we now face globally show us how much our consciousness is cut off from nature, both internally and externally. The key to change is not adjusting the system or knowledge or technology. The answer is inside us. The answer is recovering our true nature, which is harmonious and friendly, and which seeks the good of all. In these times, recovering our true nature involves restoring the harmony and peace of the earth.

Within all of us is an intense longing for the Mago Castle of old, where we once lived with a pure, free, and peaceful consciousness in oneness with nature. Quiet your mind, control your breathing, and feel the beating of your heart. You will remember the Vow of Bokbon echoing within you, the pledge to recover your lost true nature and return to Mago Castle. The great dream and longing for a world where all are one will revive. The heart that prays for the happiness and well-being of all things and all people will revive. And the mind of the Earth Citizen will revive.

Make Life a Work of Art

A song I enjoy listening to lately is a Korean song entitled "In the Brightest Place in the World, in the Most Brilliant Voice." It's a song that encourages us to ponder the meaning of life. I'd like to interpret the meaning of the song for you.

> *As once-green leaves vanish without a trace,*
> *A cold wind blows and another year is over.*
> *On the path that leads to the campus*
> *My dreams are silently lined up.*
> *Sometimes, I wandered without signposts*
> *And I even tackled the walls of life that never stop coming.*
> *Even if my greatest hopes remain as dreams,*
> *What I can achieve is also in those dreams.*

Once-green leaves vanishing and a cold wind blowing signify time flowing by. We generally have dreams in our school years, when some of our purity remains as yet untainted by the world. As we grow older, those dreams gradually fade. We want to realize our dreams, but we wander and run into walls of despair. The secret to being able to hold on to the thread of our hopes, no matter how difficult life may become, is found in our dreams. If we give up even our dreams, though we live, we are not alive. Though young, a person without a dream isn't youthful. Conversely, even older people overflow with the vigorous energy of youth if they have a dream.

That's why dreams make us young and healthy.

The song continues:

The way we are now can never come again.
Everyone is like that, and goodbyes await us all.

Once today is gone, the way we are now will never come again. We can't avoid the separation that comes to everyone. Our final parting is death. Money, power, and fame are meaningless before death. It is because of death that they say life is suffering and meaningless. But death is a blessing for those who know it is a great design that allows us to realize the completion of our souls. Because death awaits us, we think, "How should I live to live well now?" For we know that we cannot just live out our lives according to our emotions, according to our desires. How should we live while death is staring us in the face? This song offers us the following answer.

May we achieve our precious dreams
to protect our pureness as we keep faith in the Truth.
May we sing our goodbyes in the most brilliant voices in the world.
In the brightest place in the world may we sing of our reunion.

The key is to avoid losing your desire to believe the truth and to protect your purity, the desire to realize your dreams. This is a life of pursuing oneness with the Tao. The most brilliant voices in the brightest place in the world means our bright consciousness. It's important to realize that we have a mind like the Bon Shim Bon Tae Yang—our original mind, bright as the sun—that is spoken of in the Chun Bu Kyung. Although death takes our bodies, not even it can take away that bright consciousness. If you tremble in fear before death, death will swallow up those fearful emotions. However, if you can say, "Oh, there comes death now. Welcome. Yeah, I've been waiting for you," your soul will feel true freedom.

I want you to feel the bright energy inside you and to continue developing that feeling through practice. And I want you to continue designing your life using that bright energy. There will be things that the life force inside you wants to express through you. Discover them and express them. Awaken to the substance of the life inside you, and create reality through the bright light of the Tao. Creation is not difficult. All you have to do is feel the life energy inside you and express it, going with the flow. Life is short, as Hippocrates said, and art is long. A life spent discovering and creating the light of the Tao, the great light of life, is itself a work of art.

> Discovering and creating the light of the Tao is itself a work of art.

The Tao artist doesn't just hack away at something however she wants, without being centered. Infinite creation is possible for her because she has a definite center. That center is her *principles*. They are principles that come from a place deep in her life. A centered person is not shaken. When they are centered, our minds can pursue genuine love and harmony that are completely open in every direction.

Your life energy, the energy of your soul, is expressed through your face in a smile, through your mouth in affirmation and praise, through your eyes in looks of love and assurance, and through your hands in healing actions. All actions that use the energy of the soul are the light and colors of hope that heal you, those around you, and the world. Go forward together, using that light and those colors to paint a beautiful, harmonious landscape.

And later, when you are older and facing death, I want you to be able to write a poem as you look back on your life. One who can write a poem and sing a song before death is a true artist. I want you to go on creating your life, making it into one that allows you to boldly and confidently welcome death within great, bright consciousness.

You have a soul that can share pure love, a brain capable of infinite creation, and dazzling life energy—the sign of unconditional love and blessings. What do you have to worry about then? Be grateful for and love everything. Become a wonderful Tao artist who speaks of hope every moment and sings to the world.

We are one.
We are completely one within life energy.
Our love will continue.
Our creation will also continue.
Our lives will be eternal together with eternal life energy.
The hope you have been seeking is breathing in your life.
Make your life and the world beautiful by coloring them with that life energy.
That is the living Tao.

Thank you for taking a jouney to the Tao with me.
If you feel a flower of the Tao blossom in your heart,
please share it with others.

ACKNOWLEGMENTS

I would like to acknowlege the creative team at Best Life Media: Hyerin Moon, Jiyoung Oh, and Michela Mangiaracina for their support in organizing the material and producing this book. I would also like to express my gratidude to Daniel Graham for translating my orignal Korean manuscript into English, and to Nicole Dean, Wendy Oden, and Lesley Dahl for their thoughtful editing throughout all stages of this book.

ABOUT THE AUTHOR

Ilchi Lee is an impassioned visionary, educator, mentor, and innovator; he has dedicated his life to teaching energy principles and researching and developing methods to nurture the full potential of the human brain.

For over thirty years, his life's mission has been to help people harness their own creative power and personal potential. For this goal, he has developed many successful mind-body training methods, including Body & Brain Yoga and Brain Education. His principles and methods have inspired many people around the world to live healthier and happier lives.

Lee is a *New York Times* bestselling author who has penned thirty-eight books, including *The Call of Sedona: Journey of the Heart*, *Change: Realizing Your Greatest Potential*, and *Brain Wave Vibration: Getting Back into the Rhythm of a Happy, Healthy Life.*

He is also a well-respected humanitarian who has been working with the United Nations and other organizations for global peace. Lee serves as the president of the University of Brain Education and the International Brain Education Association. For more information about Ilchi Lee and his work, visit ilchi.com. To learn his methods of personal development online, visit www.ChangeYourEnergy.com.